THE IMPORTANCE OF
BEING HUMAN

Number Eleven
BAMPTON LECTURES IN AMERICA
Delivered at Columbia University 1958

THE IMPORTANCE OF
BEING HUMAN

SOME ASPECTS OF
THE CHRISTIAN DOCTRINE OF MAN

By E. L. MASCALL

GREENWOOD PRESS, PUBLISHERS
WESTPORT, CONNECTICUT

Library of Congress Cataloging in Publication Data

Mascall, Eric Lionell, 1905-
  The importance of being human.

    Reprint of the ed. published by Columbia University
Press, New York, which was issued as no. 11 of
Bampton lectures in America.
    Bibliography: p.
    1. Man (Theology) I. Title. II. Series:
Bampton lectures in America, no. 11.
[BT701.2.M365 1974]   233   74-12849
ISBN 0-8371-7761-8

Originally published in 1958 by Columbia University Press,
New York

Reprinted with the permission of Columbia University Press

Reprinted in 1974 by Greenwood Press, Inc.
51 Riverside Avenue, Westport, CT 06880

Library of Congress catalog card number 74-12849
ISBN 0-8371-7761-8

Printed in the United States of America

10 9 8 7 6 5 4 3 2

FOREWORD

Whatever judgement may be passed on the manner of its treatment, it will hardly be denied that the subject which I have chosen for this book—man, his nature, his end, his predicament, his resources—is of peculiar relevance at the present day, when the human race is confronted simultaneously with greater possibilities of material achievement and with greater dangers to its very existence than at any other time in its recorded history. A note of irony is added by the fact that Christian theologians themselves are far from agreement upon the basic issues, though it is to be hoped that sympathetic discussion may reveal their divergences to be less than they have sometimes thought them to be. Indeed, I am not without hope that the present book, which was originally delivered as the Bampton Lectures for 1958 at Columbia University in the City of New York, may contribute in some degree to this much to be desired *rapprochement*. The situation being what it is, however, it may be well to make it plain at the outset that the standpoint from which the subject is discussed is that of a Catholic theologian of the Anglican allegiance.

When, by the legacy which he left at his death in 1751,

the Reverend John Bampton founded in the University of Oxford the divinity lectureship which bears his name, he prudently ordained that no person should ever be Bampton Lecturer more than once. Dying as he did a quarter of a century before the American Declaration of Independence, the benevolent prebendary of Salisbury was not in a position to foresee that his praiseworthy prohibition would be even more laudably vitiated by the munificence of a kinswoman who long after his death would provide, with those differences appropriate to the changes of time and place, that Bampton Lectures should be delivered in the New World as well as in the Old. It is thus through the generosity of the late Mrs. Ada Byron Bampton Tremaine and the courteous invitation of Columbia University that I have been enabled to appear in the hitherto unknown role of the man who has been Bampton Lecturer twice.

E. L. M.

New York
May, 1958

ACKNOWLEDGEMENTS

Acknowledgement for permission to quote is due George Allen and Unwin, for *Evolution as a Process*, edited by Julian S. Huxley and others; Geoffrey Bles, for *The Screwtape Letters*, by Clive Staples Lewis; Chatto and Windus, for *The Uniqueness of Man*, by Julian S. Huxley; James Clarke, for *The Mystical Theology of the Eastern Church*, by Vladimir Lossky, translated by members of the Fellowship of St. Alban and St. Sergius; The Dacre Press (A. & C. Black), for *Revelation and the Modern World*, by Lionel Spencer Thornton; John Day, for *The Future of Industrial Man*, by Peter F. Drucker; The Macmillan Company, for *Scholasticism and Politics*, by Jacques Maritain, translated by Mortimer J. Adler; Pantheon Books, for *The Silence of St. Thomas*, by Josef Pieper, translated by John Murray and Daniel O'Connor; and Sheed and Ward, for *A Philosophy of Work*, by Etienne Borne and François Henry, translated by Francis Jackson, for *The Spirit of Medieval Philosophy*, by Etienne Gilson, translated by A. H. C. Downes, for *Religion and Culture*, by Jacques Maritain, translated by J. F. Scanlan; also Scribner's for *The Spirit of Medieval Philosophy*, by Etienne Gilson.

CONTENTS

Note: Biblical quotations are mostly given in the text of the American Revised Standard Version

I · THE UNIQUENESS OF MAN

What is man that thou art mindful of him, or the son of man, that thou carest for him? Thou didst make him for a little while lower than the angels, thou hast crowned him with glory and honour, putting everything in subjection under his feet.[1]

Whether or not there are rational beings in some part or parts of the material universe other than that which we inhabit—and this is a question whose implications for Christian theology I have discussed in another place [2]—science and theology would agree in holding that, on this planet at least, man is unique. It does not, however, necessarily follow from this that they would agree on the kind of uniqueness which each would ascribe to him, or even that these two kinds of uniqueness are compatible. This chapter is therefore devoted to the question of the uniqueness of man.

To the scientifically uneducated patron of science fiction, whose knowledge of biology has hardly progressed beyond the stage of the schoolboy who said that the theory of evolution means that monkeys are descended from Darwin, and whose mind is haunted by pictures of colossal ants with electronic calculators instead of brains, it may come as something of a surprise to be told that, even from the scientific

point of view, man is a highly special and remarkable phe-
nomenon and that rational beings are not at all the sort of
things that you would expect to find just any place. To be-
gin with, the environments in which life, whether rational
or irrational, can flourish are very specialised environments.
In the colder parts of the universe there is not enough energy to sustain living beings, and in the hotter parts all
chemical molecules have decomposed and indeed the very
atoms themselves are stripped of their electrons. Furthermore, if we may assume that life—or at any rate, life of
anything but the very humblest type—needs an atmosphere
which contains plenty of oxygen but very little methane or
ammonia, certain rather delicate and improbable relations
need to be satisfied between the mass of a planet and its
temperature throughout the course of its history if it is to
provide a suitable theatre for biological evolution. Otherwise it will either have lost all its oxygen or it will have
retained, with its oxygen, its methane and ammonia.

How common such favourable environments are is a
difficult question whose answer depends on highly contro-
versial aspects of cosmology and planetary theory. Whether
planetary systems are normal accompaniments of stars or
whether they are highly exceptional freaks which require
for their formation an improbable concatenation of circumstances, such as the very close passing-by of another massive
body, is a matter on which contemporary astronomers are
far from having reached agreement. In 1928 the late Sir
Arthur Eddington would admit only that there might be "a
few rival earths dotted here and there about the universe." [3]
However, since that date our conception of the number
of possible methods of planetary evolution has been much

enlarged, and some of these methods would make possible sites for life comparatively common. It is now claimed that something like a thousand million extragalactic nebulae are accessible to observation [4] and that each of them may contain something like a hundred thousand million stars; [5] so that, even if we suppose that the formation of a planetary system around a star is a *relatively* infrequent affair—and this is itself a very questionable assumption—the *total* possible number of sites for life may be very large indeed. Thus, in 1955 Fred Hoyle, on the basis of his most recent theory of planetary evolution, affirmed that there might be as many as a hundred thousand million planetary systems in our galaxy alone.[6]

It would not, of course, follow that all these sites, or even all those in which the conditions were favourable for life, were in fact inhabited, though most scientists, on the strength of recent investigations by virologists in the border region between non-living and living matter, would be inclined to say that nature has a dislike for unoccupied sites and that life arises wherever the environment is hospitable to it. Nor would it follow that, even where biological evolution had taken place, this had necessarily culminated in the appearance of beings with rational powers or (as Christianity holds to be the case in man) with a supracosmic destiny. Nevertheless, the fact remains that there is no scientific ground for asserting that nowhere in the material universe except upon this earth of ours is there to be found a rational organic being. Nor, I have argued elsewhere,[7] is there any conclusive ground for such an assertion in Christian dogma; that is not, however, the point with which we are concerned at the moment. What we have seen is that, if man is certainly unique, it must be with more than a merely numerical uniqueness. And this, in fact, appears to be the case.

The unwary reader of books on popular biology can easily form in his mind the picture of the evolutionary tree as a kind of bush with no discernible central trunk but with a proliferation of ever dividing and subdividing shoots whose terminations at any particular epoch are all on much the same footing, although some of them are bacteria and some of them amoebae, some nettles, some tigers, and some men. He would admit that these different terminals are not on *exactly* the same footing, but he would see no significant differences between the various processes that have led to each of them and he would see no reason why, given a suitable environment and a sufficient number of millennia, the bacterial or tigritic stocks should not ultimately count among their members rational beings, although rational beings of a very different physical structure from that possessed by men. The superintelligent giant ant or the hyper-tapeworm composing four-dimensional music for the electron-wave trombone would seem to him to be a perfectly possible evolutionary form. However, as Julian Huxley has pointed out in a fascinating essay whose title I have stolen for the present chapter,[8] there are very strong biological and physical reasons for supposing that any being which is able to do the sort of things that man does must possess the same general sort of bodily structure that man possesses. In Huxley's words:

The course followed by evolution appears to have been broadly as follows. From a generalised early type, various lines radiate out, exploiting the environment in various ways. Some of these comparatively soon reach a limit to their evolution, at least as regards major alteration. Thereafter they are limited to minor changes such as the formation of new genera and species. Others, on the other hand, are so constructed that they can continue their career, generating new types which are successful in the struggle for existence because of their greater control over the environment and their greater independence of it. Such changes are legitimately called "progressive." The new type repeats the process. It radiates out into a number of lines, each specialising in a particular direction. The great majority of these come up against dead ends and can advance no further; specialisation is a one-sided process. . . .

Sometimes all the branches of a given stock have come up against their limit, and then either have become extinct or have persisted without major change. . . .

In other cases, all but one or two of the lines suffer this fate, while the rest repeat the process. All reptilian lines were blind alleys save two—one which was transformed into the birds, and another which became the mammals. Of the bird stock, all lines came to a dead end; of the mammals, all but one—the one which became man.

Thus, Huxley tells us,

Evolution is . . . seen as an enormous number of blind alleys, with a very occasional path of progress. It is like a maze in which almost all turnings are wrong turnings. The goal of the evolutionary maze, however, is not a central chamber, but a road which will lead indefinitely onwards.[9]

The reasons why so many of the turnings were blind alleys are not difficult to understand. Thus, for example, owing to the fact that the bulk of an organism is proportional to the cube of its linear dimensions while its surface area is proportional to the square, it is impossible for a given type to reach more than a certain size if it relies for respiration upon direct surface absorption of oxygen. It simply will not be able to take in enough oxygen to keep its muscles and other organs going; for if you double the linear dimensions, you multiply the surface by four and the volume by eight, and so the ratio of surface to volume is halved. This is why the giant insects of science fiction are a biological impossibility. And since the higher mental processes require a brain mechanism with a large number of brain cells for their exercise, there can be no real evolutionary prospect for the insect world.

The future lay, in fact, with the land vertebrates, and in particular with those—the mammals and the birds—which achieved, through their mechanism of temperature regulation, that basic stability which is essential for a consistent mental life. The birds, however, ran into a blind alley in their turn, mainly through overspecialising their forelimbs for the functions of flight; and many of the mammals fell victims to other forms of specialisation. Only a being who was first arboreal and later terrestrial could develop the manipulative hands which provide man with his power over other organisms, both animal and vegetable. And only one who was gregarious and uniparous could become the subject of an intelligent social life. Thus, to quote Huxley again:

We are now in a position to define the uniqueness of human evolution. The essential character of man as a dominant organism is conceptual thought. And conceptual thought could have arisen only in a multicellular animal, an animal with bilateral symmetry, head and blood system, a vertebrate as against a mollusc or an arthropod, a land vertebrate among vertebrates, a mammal among land vertebrates. Finally, it could have arisen only in a mammalian line which was gregarious, which produced one young at a birth instead of several, and which had recently become terrestrial after a long period of arboreal life.

Huxley is quite definite about his conclusions:

There is only one group of animals which fulfils these conditions
—a terrestrial offshoot of the higher Primates. Thus not merely
has conceptual thought been evolved only in man: it could not
have been evolved except in man. There is but one path of unlimited progress through the evolutionary maze. The course of
human evolution is as unique as its result. . . . Conceptual
thought on this planet is inevitably associated with a particular
type of Primate body and Primate brain.[10]

Père Teilhard de Chardin has gone into even more detail:

All the metamorphosis leading up to man reduces, from the organic standpoint, to the question of producing a better brain. But
how could this perfecting of the brain have been produced, how
could it have taken place, unless a whole series of other conditions had been realised all together and at once? If the being
which issued in man had not been a biped, his hands would not
have found themselves free to take over the prehensile functions
from the jaws, and so the thick bundle of maxillary muscles
which constricted the skull would not have been relaxed. It is
thanks to the liberation of the hands through the adoption of
biped movement that the brain has been able to grow, and also
that the eyes have been able to draw together, across the nar-
rowed face, and so to converge and "fix" whatever the hands
may have grasped, brought near and, in every sense of the word,
presented: the very outward gesture of reflection.[11]

Quite recently this position has been argued with great
emphasis from the standpoint of the youthful sciences of
biocybernetics and the theory of servo-mechanisms by Albert Ducrocq in his book *The Origins of Life.* And the
immensity of the gulf which separates even the most primitive men from the most highly developed subhuman beings
has been strikingly demonstrated by Leslie Paul in his re-

cent book *Nature into History*, in which a great amount
of anthropological material is gathered together and its implications for this thesis are shown.

It must now be pointed out that, from the scientific point
of view at least, the arrival of man does not mean that the
evolutionary process has come to an end. What it does mean
is that it has reached a turning-point of the most novel and
far-reaching kind. For an intelligent being is able to take
in hand and direct the evolutionary process itself, not only
as it is manifested in animal and vegetable species but as it
is manifested in his own. To quote Huxley again:

> The human type became a microcosm which, through its ca-
> pacities for awareness, was able to incorporate increasing amounts
> of the macrocosm into itself, to organise them in new and richer
> ways, and then with their aid to exert new and more powerful
> influences on the macrocosm. And the present situation represents
> a further highly remarkable point in the development of our
> planet—the critical point at which the evolutionary process, as
> now embodied in man, has for the first time become aware of
> itself, is studying the laws of its own unfolding, and has a dawn-
> ing realisation of the possibilities of its future guidance or control.
> In other words, evolution is on the verge of becoming internal-
> ised, conscious, and self-directing.[12]

> Progress has hitherto been a rare and fitful by-product of evo-
> lution. Man has the possibility of making it the main feature of
> his own future evolution, and of guiding its course in relation to a
> deliberate aim.[13]

I shall not here follow up the truly exhilarating and at
the same time terrifying possibilities that are opened up by
these last considerations. I shall instead inquire how we are
to understand this particular kind of uniqueness of man to

which Huxley has drawn attention, which is manifested in
the fact that, of all the paths that can be traced in the evolutionary process, there is only one that has not led to the
dead-end of stalemate or extinction, and that this is the path
that has led up to man. And we might perhaps remark in
passing that C. S. Lewis would seem to be keeping closer
to scientific truth when, in his novels *Out of the Silent
Planet* and *Perelandra,* he endows his inhabitants of Mars
and Venus with human or quasi-human bodies and minds,
than is J. K. Heydon in his *World D,* with its geometrical
and radioactive Triangulans and its excessively sensitive and
sensual Purple Cygnians with their sixty legs and their Blue
and White wives. Before leaving the point we might, however, raise the question whether Huxley, in arguing that intelligent mental life is necessarily tied up with the possession of a body substantially like ours, may not have been
assuming without proof certain hypotheses that are not altogether certain. Given the assumption that mental life is possible only in association with nerve cells of the kind that we
find in terrestrial animals, the rest of his argument seems to
follow smoothly and convincingly; but can we be quite
sure that this assumption is true? No reasons have been
given, either for or against, and I suggest that the question
should be left open. It will be more to the point to inquire
whether the fact that, in Huxley's words, "there is but one
path of unlimited progress through the evolutionary maze,"
namely, the path that leads to man, can be interpreted as the
sign of a conscious purpose, such as a theist might identify
with the immanent working of God.

We ought, I suggest, to be very careful how we make such
an identification. A theist will, of course, see every event

that occurs as being ultimately due to God's creative activity, whether he can discern any obvious purposiveness in it or not. There are, however, several reasons why he ought to hesitate before ascribing any immediate theistic significance to apparently purposeful processes in nature.

There are, for example, features in the evolutionary process which, if they are taken as *prima facie* evidence for a conscious design, might well seem to suggest that the designer is incompetent, casual, or even malevolent. The Christian has indeed an explanation of the existence of these features, in terms of rebellion against the Creator on the part of creatures, both angelic and human. But just because he describes the features in those terms he is precluded from holding that every appearance of design is to be identified, immediately and without qualification, with the creative activity of God. The difficulty with all approaches to theism which are based upon cosmic teleology is that the chief objection to the teleological argument—namely, the problem of evil—is only resolved after the goal of the argument has been reached. There is, however, a more fundamental objection than this, the objection which alleges that the appearance of purpose is itself an illusion.

It is well known that Darwinism achieved its great *succès de scandale* by its claim to eliminate from the universe all the evidences of design. As originally formulated, the Darwinian theory rested upon three presuppositions: that of random variations, that of natural selection, and that of the inheritance of acquired characters. In its original form the theory has been abandoned. Random variations appear to be neither significant nor inheritable. There are, however, much more significant changes, known as mutations, which are inherited according to the so-called Mendelian laws. Whether the inheritance of mutations *plus* the operation of natural selection are sufficient to account for the evolutionary changes that actually occur is a matter of controversy among biologists. The symposium *Evolution as a Process*, which appeared in 1954 and was written by a number of very eminent biologists—and which contained one of the essays by Huxley from which I have quoted in this chapter —vigorously defended the sufficiency of natural selection. In particular, the distinguished geneticist and statistician Sir Ronald Fisher argued that even very slightly advantageous variations may, after a number of generations, produce changes of a magnitude that it might have seemed previously quite impossible to ascribe to anything other than deliberate design.

It is true that the theist will ascribe to the ultimate activity of God the central process that winds through the maze of evolutionary bifurcations and terminates in man, but then he will also ascribe to the same ultimate and august activity the blind alleys that terminate in ants and squids and cuckoos. If we are going to interpret the process theistically, we must take it as a whole; it will not do to single out one strand and concentrate on that to the neglect of the fabric. What we have to do is to view the whole evolutionary process and the place which man holds in it, and then ask ourselves whether and in what way we can interpret this as manifesting God's purpose for man. This does not necessarily mean that we shall base our belief in God's existence upon our examination of the cosmic process; that may well have come to us from other sources before we started. But it does mean that when we bring our belief in God to the interpretation of the cosmic process we shall contemplate that process as a whole and not just one part of it. And so our question is this: how are we to interpret the process of evolution, and man as implicated in it, in the light of the Christian doctrine about both God and man?

Christian theologians have often asserted that the significance of man is to be judged by what he is and not by how he has come to be; and this assertion is, so far as it goes, a good one. As William Temple once remarked, "I am greater than the stars, for I know that they are up there and they do not know that I am down here." Nevertheless, the fact cannot be altogether ignored that, when we consider the evolutionary process from the scientific point of view, man's appearance on the scene does seem to be very much a matter of chance, even if the scale of the game is so big that the chance was one which sooner or later was, as we say, "bound to come off." Granted that in a universe containing something like a hundred million million million stars there are bound to be a number of planets which will provide a suitable environment for life, and granted that on some of them a line of development will successfully thread its way through the evolutionary maze without getting extinguished on the way and will finally culminate in an organism with a structure like that of the higher primates, does this really allow us to believe that the final product—man—is the object of God's solicitude and purpose in the way in which the Christian Church has always envisaged him, as stamped with God's image and set by God over the rest of creation, crowned with glory and honour and with all things in subjection under his feet? After all, the very mutations which play such an essential part in the process of evolution are, so we are told, the result of quantum changes which, even if in the aggregate they can be brought under statistical generalisations, are individually a matter of pure chance. In such a universe does not man, for all his admitted uniqueness, appear as one of those occasional oddities—like the hand at cards which consists of a complete suit—which are bound to turn up sooner or later if you set going a sufficient number of random processes and let them proceed for a long enough time, as in fact the product of chance rather than of design? We can imagine the hand which was all hearts preening itself on its superlative order and beauty and convincing itself that it must have been deliberately planned by the dealer, whereas in fact it was (it is to be hoped) no more planned than any other hand which he had ever dealt. To change the metaphor, the picture of man which science puts before us would seem to be simply the picture of the successful cosmic bandit, the character who, by a happy combination of good fortune and adroitness, has carved out for himself in the universe a position of prominence and affluence for which he can plead no official authorisation or backing, and whose ultimate fate is a matter of complete indifference to the supreme administrative authority, if indeed any such authority exists. In fact, one of the tragedies of the scientific humanism which is the implicit or explicit philosophy of most educated Anglo-Saxons is that it sees man as occupying a position of unprecedented achievement and at the same time as having no guarantee for his future, either here or beyond the grave. Has the Christian theologian a reply to make to this? Can he, if he honestly faces the universe of science, retain his belief in the providence of God? I believe he can, if he is true to his theology.

First, we must remember that, according to traditional Christian belief, a man is not just a highly developed biological organism, but a highly developed biological organism which has been subsumed into a mysterious and complicated union with a spiritual and immortal soul; and this is as true of our primeval human ancestors as of ourselves. Even if we hold that the production of man's body is a matter of "pure chance" (and I shall take up that point farther on) the production of *man* is not a matter of chance, if it involves the direct and deliberate action of God. In the language of Genesis, "The Lord God formed man of dust from the ground, and breathed into his nostrils the breath of life," [14] and, however the original writer understood his assertion, there is nothing to prevent us from taking the "dust from the ground" as denoting one of the higher anthropoids. The production of this anthropoid may indeed be a matter of chance, like so much in the evolutionary process, but need that worry us? Suppose that God uses just this method of "chance" to produce here and there the occasional physical organism which, by its organic adaptability and its cerebral complexity, is an adequate counterpart for a rational and spiritual soul. No doubt this method will seem disgracefully wasteful to the economical mind of bourgeois man, who will expect a God to whom all things are possible to reach his ends in a more businesslike and simpler way. However, God, unlike man, is not limited in his resources and has no need to be governed by considerations of economy. If he is self-existent Goodness and if *bonum est diffusivum sui,* may we not think of him as tossing off in the sheer joy of creation such trifles as galaxies, in vast excess of what is strictly necessary for the fulfilment of his ultimate purpose of creating man? And God is in any case glorified by the "dead ends"—the dinosaurs, the ants, and the bacteria—as well as by the "main-line" organisms which are in the direct ancestry of man. (May I make it plain in passing that I am not maintaining that nothing has gone wrong in the evolutionary process. If something has gone wrong, it is the doing of rebellious finite beings; and if it hampers, it does not bring to a standstill, the achievement of God's aims.) Perhaps some modern apologists have gone badly astray in looking for direct evidences of God's design in the evolutionary process. The truth may be that God is able to achieve his ends without that sort of design. It is at least worthy of notice that "cosmic teleology" is a modern feature in Christian apologetics; it is not found, for example, in St. Thomas Aquinas. And I suspect it is the product of a commercially minded age.

Second, we must remember that, for Christian theism, no events are fortuitous or chance events in the ultimate metaphysical sense, and that nothing happens without an ultimate metaphysical cause. In the words of St. Thomas Aquinas:

A thing can escape from the control of a particular cause, but not from that of the universal cause. . . . So far, then, as any effect escapes the control of some particular cause it is said to be casual or fortuitous in relation to that particular cause, but in relation to the universal cause, from whose control it cannot be withdrawn, it is said to be foreseen. Thus, for example, the meeting of two servants, although it may be fortuitous so far as they are concerned, has nevertheless been foreseen by their master, if he has deliberately sent them to the same place without letting either of them know about the other.[15]

Applying this consideration to our own problem, we must recognise that, even if the individual mutations which are so important a factor in biological evolution are random, indeterminate, and "uncaused" from the point of view of physical theory, this does not mean that they have escaped from the primary creative causality of God. Nor, on the other hand, if they conform in their statistical distribution to the laws of quantum theory does this mean that God has abdicated from his sovereignty over them. It is in fact one of the paradoxical features of probability laws that, while we have to derive the probabilities from the observation of sequences of occurrences, any occurrence is compatible with any postulated probability, for probability laws determine nothing whatever about any individual instance within their ambit. To put the matter less technically, what appears from the scientific point of view as chance and indeterminacy is from the theological point of view the area within which God, when laying down the limits within which secondary causes are to operate under the overarching aegis of his primary causality, has left himself free to act without reference to the pattern of secondary causes at all. Einstein once expressed his dislike of probability laws as the foundation of physics by the phrase "God doesn't play dice"; but the truth is that even those individual happenings which to the gamester or the physicist are a matter of "pure chance" are under the ultimate determination of the Creator, without whom neither a click is heard in the loud speaker attached to a Geiger counter nor a sparrow falls to the ground.

The judgement which all fundamentally naturalistic interpretations of the universe bring upon themselves is an inability to conceive the ultimate nature of the universe in other than impersonal terms. Where the theist sees human life as an exhilarating adventure of human freedom played out under the fatherly oversight of the divine providence, the secularist sees it as a grim domain of fate from which the only possible escape is provided by luck or chance; as a dyarchy of *ananke* and *tyche*, of *fatum* and *fortuna*. Like the apostate Jews in the days of the second Isaiah, he prepares a table for Fortune and fills up mingled wine unto Destiny.[16] And the difference is in the last resort that, while freedom and providence are personal terms, Destiny and Fortune—fate and chance—are impersonal, even when they are metaphorically personified as gods or goddesses. We need not worry that science describes the course of evolution in impersonal concepts; that is its job. Nor need we worry that God's creation has its impersonal aspects, for even God's own personality does not annihilate the impersonal but transcends and subsumes it. What is reprehensible is any attempt to treat the scientific account as if it were a metaphysical one, to transport the impersonality of science into the metaphysical realm.

In the modern Anglo-Saxon world, or at any rate in my own country, we are, it seems to me, in the almost diametrically opposite position to that of the Church in the ancient world. It was the perennial failing of ancient religion that it tended to see the personal everywhere, to identify everything with the divine, to worship everything within sight—stones and cats and crocodiles. It is the radical defect of Western twentieth-century civilisation, on the other hand, that it tends to depersonalise everything, even the ultimate ground of existence, the great First Cause of which St. Thomas could still say in his day that all men understood it to be God.[17] In the ancient world the Church had to devote a large amount of its effort to stopping people from worshipping, for polytheism was for them almost second nature. In our time the Church finds it difficult to get people to understand the very notion of worship, and the civilised European —I must leave you to decide whether this is true of the civilised American as well—is as little likely to become a polytheist as to become a Polynesian.

This discussion, however, must come to an end. What I have tried to do in this first chapter is to show that, in spite of the radical difference of the scientific approach from that of theology, there is nothing in the history of the human race as it is envisaged by evolutionary biology which need lead us to abandon the traditional belief of Christendom that man is the uniquely favoured creature upon whom God has stamped his own image, crowning him with glory and honour and putting all things in subjection under his feet, true as it is that we do not yet see everything in subjection to him.

II · BODY AND SOUL

I noted in the last chapter the difficulty which civilised Western man in the world of today experiences in convincing
himself that he has any special assigned status in the universe,
and upon the sense of instability which this uncertainty produces. Many of the psychological disorders which are so
common and distressing a feature of our time are, I believe,
to be traced to this cause. No less is the difficulty that man
has in believing that he is a being of a definite and determinate nature—indeed, the difficulty may well be greater.
So long as his thought was nourished on the concepts of
Greek philosophy the matter was pretty plain. In Greek
thought, every being in the universe belonged to some species
or other, every species had its own sharply defined nature,
and man was no exception to this rule: he was the rational
or the reasoning animal. The changes through which a human being passed from infancy to maturity merely marked
the passage from an imperfect to a perfect manifestation
of the specific nature of man; and the differences which
could be seen between one adult man and another were sub-
specific individual differentiae of no special importance. In
spite of the tremendous transformation which Christianity

worked upon the notion of finite beings in general and of human beings in particular—a transformation some of whose aspects we shall be considering later on—the fundamental outlook was unchanged. Man was a being of a particular kind, although a highly unique one; what that kind was he could know by reason and revelation; and his duty and his beatitude consisted in living as the kind of being that he was, in accordance with the laws of his nature. It was his duty to be human, and there was no particular difficulty in finding out what being human meant.

We are in a very different situation today. The doctrine of evolution introduced the notion that species are essentially mutable, and made no exception in the case of man. It is true, of course, that present-day biology, with its substitution of mutations for variations as the main basis for evolutionary change, does not look upon species as being quite as fluid as they were held to be in the early days of Darwinism. Furthermore, as we have seen, evolutionary processes have a way of running into dead-end situations in which a species becomes either static or extinct; and, although we cannot describe the path that leads up to man as having resulted in a dead-end in the pejorative sense of that term—it is, for example, Julian Huxley's contention that man is the supreme example of an evolutionary product that is *not* a dead-end—there seem to be strong indications that with man the evolutionary process has come to at least a relatively stationary point. Le Gros Clark writes:

The size of the brain in proportion to the body-weight is . . . one of the distinctive features of human anatomy. Its weight is two or three times that of the largest ape, the gorilla, and it seems to have taken a matter of several million years for man to achieve such a prodigious development of his brain. On the other hand, the fossil evidence indicates that the human brain has not appreciably changed in its size for about 200,000 years. There seems to be no evidence that man's brain is undergoing any further evolutionary expansion—or that it is even likely to do so.[1]

Furthermore, even the production of new species in the sub-human realm seems to be very much more a matter of faith than of observation.[2] Nevertheless, there are two points to be remembered. The first is that, whatever may be the convictions of present-day biologists, the general impression in the mind of people today is that the human species as we know it is merely one step on the way to a superhuman or trans-human series of beings, which may be more noble or more ruthless than man but will at any rate be more powerful and intelligent. Second—and this is more important for our purpose here—even if the process of natural evolution has come to a virtual full stop with the arrival of a rational species, the very arrival of that species opens up the prospect of a vastly accelerated and amplified evolutionary development of an entirely new kind, that is to say, a development which will be consciously and deliberately planned by the rational species itself. In Julian Huxley's words:

Once the critical point was passed at which conceptual thought and true speech could develop, a new method of evolution became possible—the method of cultural transformation, based upon the cumulative transmission of experience. . . .

And the present situation represents a further highly remarkable point in the development of our planet—the critical point at which the evolutionary process, as now embodied in man, has for

the first time become aware of itself, is studying the laws of its
own unfolding, and has a dawning realisation of the possibilities
of its future guidance or control. In other words, evolution is on
the verge of becoming internalised, conscious and self-directing.[3]

If this is the case, then the question of man's future is of
more than speculative importance. As long as man's development was conceived as the effect of purely external influences over which he himself had little or no control, it might
be interesting to speculate whether the human race would
be changed into something vastly different, but there
seemed to be nothing very much that man could do about
it one way or the other. If, however, it is, or very soon will
be, in man's own power to modify drastically his own genetic
material, the question whether man is to remain man or is
to be changed into something else becomes of immediate
practical moment. If the Christian religion is true, we have
quite solid reasons for holding that, whatever developments
man is meant to undergo—and these may indeed be far-
reaching—man is meant to remain man; for, if God has himself become man in the Incarnation, he has sealed human
nature with a certificate of value whose validity cannot be
disputed. This is a question to which I shall return in detail later on. At the moment I wish to stress that, whatever
may have been the case in the ancient world, with its belief
in fixed and determinate natures, we are hardly likely in the
modern world to retain our belief in the inalienable value
of man as man unless we hold that, in some way or another,
that value has been supernaturally certified.

Josef Pieper has made this point with great penetration in
his brilliant little book *The Silence of St. Thomas*, in which
he points out that for the Angelic Doctor there is a direct

link between the notion that things have natures and the
notion that they are the products of a form-giving thought.

This interrelation [he tells us] is foreign to modern Rationalism.
. . . Modern thinking habits can make nothing of the suggestion
that there could be no such "nature" unless it were thus creatively
thought. Curiously enough, this thesis of St. Thomas has received
unexpected and emphatic support in the principles of modern, indeed we might term it post-modern, Existentialism. From Sartre's
radical negation of the idea of creation (he declares, for example,
that "Existentialism is nothing more than an attempt to draw all
the conclusions from a consistently atheistic position,") it is sud-
denly made evident how and to what extent the doctrine of creation is the concealed but basic foundation of classical Western
metaphysics. If one were to compare the thought of Sartre and
St. Thomas and reduce both to syllogistic form, one would real-
ise that both start with the same "major premise", namely from
this principle: things have an essential nature only in so far as
they are fashioned by thought. . . . Then, Sartre continues, because there exists *no* creative intelligence which could have designed man and all natural things . . . therefore there is *no*
"nature" in things that are not manufactured and artificial. Here
are his actual words: "There is no such thing as human nature
because there exists no God to think it creatively." . . . St.
Thomas, on the contrary, declares: Because and in so far as God
has creatively thought things, just so and to that extent have they
a nature. . . . What is common to Sartre and St. Thomas, it is
now evident, is the assumption that we can speak of the nature
of things only when they are expressly considered as *creatura*.[4]

And again:

In criticising the philosophical atheism of the eighteenth century
Sartre shows that he is in full agreement with the old doctrine of
Being. It betrays, he declares, a sad lack of clear and logical thinking, when the concept of creation is abandoned but not the habit
of talking about the "nature of things," as though on that point

nothing had changed. It is superficial, unreasonable, and even absurd to maintain that there is a "nature" of things, anterior to existence, unless one holds at the same time that things are *creatures*.[5]

If this is so, then attempts such as that of C. H. Waddington, in his book *The Scientific Attitude*, to establish man's claim to a legitimate place in the world on purely scientific grounds are doomed to failure. He may or may not be right in claiming:

Science by itself, and so far as I can see only science by itself, unadulterated by mixture with any contrary ideal, is able to provide mankind with a way of life which is, firstly, self-consistent and harmonious, and, secondly, free for the exercise of that objective reason on which our material progress depends.[6]

But in any case the task cannot even be begun unless it is first known whether it is worth while for man to continue at all and, if so, what are the essential needs and demands of human nature. And these are questions to which science cannot give an answer.

I shall therefore take it for granted that, from the standpoint of the Christian religion, human nature is something which is certified by God as inherently worth while and that, with all its variety and flexibility, it has certain definite characteristics which must be respected, preserved, and developed. Some of these characteristics are known only by revelation within the Christian tradition; others are in principle discernible by rational examination—at least, so the Christian tradition affirms. But the Christian tradition also affirms that the human reason is so weakened and obscured by sin that even characteristics which are discernible by rational examination in principle may not be so discernible in practice. It will therefore be simpler for our purpose if we simply discuss the nature of man as Christianity envisages it, without bothering very much to inquire how much of this might be known by that hypothetical figure, the purely natural man. And the first of these characteristics of human nature which I shall discuss is that of man's dual composition as a psycho-physical organism—a unity of body and rational soul, of flesh and spirit.

Nowhere perhaps is the contrast between Christianity and most other religions more clearly seen than in its insistence on the fact that the body of a man is an integral part of him and not merely an accidental and temporary integument. (We must, of course, remember that Judaism was the ancestor of Christianity, and Mohammedanism largely a derivative from them.) Partly this conviction was derived by Christianity from its Jewish origin, as included in the belief that God is the maker of everything, matter and spirit alike. But this conviction was confirmed and made fully explicit by reflection on the great mysteries of the Incarnation and the Resurrection, for if God has united human nature to himself in its fullness of soul and body and, after undergoing physical death in that same human nature, has returned to life again with his body transformed but not discarded, it is impossible to hold that the material element in human nature is either evil or irrelevant. So strong was the conviction in Judaism that man is, to use a phrase of the late Dom Gregory Dix, an ensouled body rather than an embodied soul, that the notion of the immortality of the soul played very little part in Jewish thought, all the stress being laid upon the resurrection of the body. And this was largely true of primitive Christian thought as well. Etienne Gilson writes:

It would probably surprise a good many modern Christians to
learn that in certain of the earliest Fathers the belief in the immortality of the soul is vague almost to nonexistence. . . . A
Christianity without the immortality of the soul is not, in the long
run, absolutely inconceivable, and the proof of it is that it has
been conceived. What really would be absolutely inconceivable
would be a Christianity without the resurrection of the Man. . . .
There is no occasion therefore for surprise if certain Fathers admitted the death of soul and body pending the resurrection and
the judgment. . . . It was very soon understood, chiefly owing
to the influence of Platonism, that compelling philosophic reasons
exist for the immortality of the soul. And from that moment the
question assumed a new aspect, for now there was needed an idea
of man which would leave the immortality of the soul conceivable
and safeguard at the same time the future destiny of the body.
The Greek philosophic tradition offered a choice between two,
and only two, possible solutions of the problem, namely that of
Plato and that of Aristotle; the Christian thinkers tried first one
and then the other, and it was only after twelve centuries of
hesitation that the question was settled, when, passing quite beyond both Plato and Aristotle, medieval philosophy revealed all
its creative originality in the system of St. Thomas Aquinas.[7]

This is not the place for a panegyric upon the Angelic
Doctor, but it is worth while to note the significance of the
fact that during the twelve centuries when no philosophical
system had yet been elaborated which was adequate to
formulate and explain the Church's belief, that belief continued to be steadily held and taught with remarkably little
wavering to either side. A thoroughgoing Platonised Christianity could have held with no difficulty to the survival of
the soul, a thoroughgoing Aristotelianised Christianity could
have comfortably taught the nonexistence of the man between his death and the general resurrection, but neither
could have made real sense of the doctrine that, although the

soul continued to exist after death, the man for the time being did not, and that he would not exist again as genuinely man until soul and body were reunited. Yet this was the Church's belief, as is shown by the fact that, with an uncompromising insistence upon the events of the last day—an insistence which was almost horrifyingly exemplified by the frescos of the Last Judgement in the medieval churches—it continued without fuss to commemorate the departed at the Eucharist and to pray for the purgation of their souls against the Great Day. Those recent writers who, in reaction against a false spiritualising of the Christian religion, have maintained as the true Christian doctrine that nothing whatever remains of a man between his death and the resurrection, and have thought in terms of "collapse" and "reinflation," are simply discarding the understanding of the primitive tradition to which the Church has been led under the guidance of the Spirit and are substituting for it a doctrinaire primitivism which treats the tradition itself as a kind of fossil.

But why, it will no doubt be asked, do we need to hold that in man there is a distinct spiritual component which is not found in any sub-human creature and which is able to survive, albeit in a widowed and desolate state, the death of the body? Is such a belief simply a bit of unexorcised Platonism which has inserted itself into the Christian tradition? Why, in fact, will it not do to think in terms of collapse and reinflation? I think the answer to this question is to be seen if we ask another question, namely this: Is there any difference of kind between a man and the lower animals, between, for example, the first man and his sub-human parent? Is there in fact any real significance in the assertion of the Bible that God created man in his own image? If

we admit that God is pure Spirit and at the same time recognise that man is not a *pure* spirit but has a body which is
continuous with the rest of the material creation, have we
any real alternative, believing as we do that man is made in
the image of God, than to hold that the way in which God
made man was by uniting a physical organism—which as
a physical organism did not differ in kind from other physical organisms—with a created spirit which, without sup-
pressing the animal and vegetal functions of the physical
organism, could subsume them into and make them sub-
servient to its own supraphysical life? I would venture here
to remind you of the way in which this concept of man has
been worked out in a book which—partly because of a
rather unmanageable literary style—has never received the
wide attention which it deserves: namely Father Lionel
Thornton's largest work, *The Incarnate Lord*. To suppose
merely that man's material body has been spiritualised, in
the sense of being endowed with new capacities without being assumed into union with an existent of a higher order
than matter, is to make man different only in degree from
the beasts and is quite inadequate as an interpretation of the
great biblical declaration that God has made man in his
own image.

Thus the authentic Christian doctrine of man is not, on
the one hand, the Platonic view, which was revived at the
Renaissance by Descartes and which has been so roundly
castigated by Gilson and Jacques Maritain under the name
of "angelism"—the view that man is in his essence a pure
spirit whose inhabitation of a material body is a temporary
and, on the whole, a tiresome episode—though it must be
admitted that at certain times this view has made deep and

damaging inroads into Christianity. But neither is it, on the other hand, the view which would simply identify man with his body, and see the soul as just the epiphenomenon of a highly developed physical organism. It is the view that man is a unique and highly complicated being composed of a body which is more elaborate than, though not necessarily different from, that of any other of the primates, and a soul which, although it is in itself a purely spiritual entity, is not the kind of spirit that can function fully and freely on its own, since it is made for the express purpose of animating a material body and in fact of animating that particular human body with which it is united. From this truth a number of consequences follow.

First, it is impossible for Christianity to place any credence in that polymorphous doctrine known as Manichaeanism, which seeped in from the East in the third century and which, doctrinally if not quite certainly historically, was manifested in such bodies as the Bogomils and the Albigensians. This is the doctrine that matter is essentially evil and that therefore religion is fundamentally unconcerned with the body. It can take a variety of forms, some of which in their practical manifestations are diametrically opposed to others. For the belief that matter is evil may lead either to the conclusion that the body is an interfering and thwarting encumbrance on the soul and therefore must be crushed and bridled in the most ruthless way, or, on the other hand, to the conclusion that, since the body has a purely accidental relation to the soul, the soul cannot be seriously affected by anything that it does and that therefore it may as well be allowed to do anything it likes, however beastly and disgusting, since the soul which is the essential man will be inherently unaffected. It is important not to be misled into supposing that sensuality is always the outcome of a belief in the essential goodness of the body and all its instincts; it is just as likely to be the outcome of a belief that the body is essentially bad. Those rigid moralists, for example, who denounce the grossness of the novels of Aldous Huxley are quite mistaken if they suppose him to be a joyful and uninhibited pagan, rejoicing in the free and spontaneous revellings of the holy and glorious flesh; he is, in contrast, a disillusioned angelist, an angel *manqué*, who is venting his disgust upon the physical organism—the malodorous jumble of tubes and glands and secretions—with which he finds himself entangled and from which he cannot get away, since it is part of himself. It is therefore not surprising that he has in his later writings turned to the advocacy of Indian types of mysticism and has so enthusiastically, if somewhat prematurely, propagandized the drugs which are alleged to provide short cuts to their attainment; for it is the common feature of Indian mysticism, for all the bewildering variety of its manifestations, that it claims to provide an escape from the phenomenal world—that is, from the world of matter.

In contrast with both these extremes, the Christian tradition holds that the body is a part of the man and that matter, no less than spirit, is created by God and therefore needs neither to be crushed nor indulged, but to be sanctified. In practice genuine Christian asceticism may sometimes be as severe, or almost as severe, as any that can be found in human history, but it is sharply differentiated from all forms of Manichaeanism or quasi-Manichaeanism by the fact that its purpose is not the annihilation of the body but the sanctification of the whole man. And, in so far as it is possible to localise the seat of evil in man, Christian orthodoxy has situated it not in the body but in the soul, for, it holds, nothing can be strictly evil except the wrong decision of a created will, and the human will, although it operates in the closest union with the bodily urges and instincts, is inherently a faculty of the soul and not of the body. It is interesting to note the place which this conviction played in the Church's repudiation of one of the early heresies about the human nature of Christ. The Apollinarians of the fourth century, who taught that in Christ the place normally held in a man by the soul was occupied by the Logos, the Second Person of the Holy Trinity, urged in support of their view that the soul was the seat of sin and that therefore it was proper that the sinless Christ should not have a human soul. The orthodox Fathers, while repudiating the Apollinarian heresy, never thought of denying that the soul was the seat of sin in fallen man; on the contrary they insisted that, just because this was the case, it was necessary that Christ should possess a human soul, although a sinless one; for otherwise the very part of man which was most radically sinful would not have been redeemed.

A second consequence of the belief in the union of soul and body in man is that this makes it very hazardous to theorise *a priori* about the sort of being that man is—to try, for example, to draw detailed conclusions about his physiology or psychology from the definition of man as a rational animal. As we have seen, Julian Huxley has argued plausibly that, at any rate on this planet, a rational being will necessarily have the general physical structure that we find in ourselves. It is, however, always well to maintain a certain reserve about *a priori* demonstrations whose conclusions are known in advance; any readers who are physicists will hardly need to be reminded of some highly mysterious arguments of the late Sir Arthur Eddington.[8] And in any case, the kind of considerations that Huxley puts forward lead to only the most general features of the human frame. To be an angel is presumably a very simple business, at least if the statements of theologians about angels are to be relied upon; but to be a human being is a very complicated business indeed, for a human being is a very complicated organism. There are no doubt certain broad truths that we can derive from the basic fact of man's composite nature as a unity of body and spirit, and there are certain vitally important facts concerning him which we know about by divine revelation; but for all the details of his peculiar physiology and psychology we are bound to depend upon empirical investigation.

A very large amount of human suffering and frustration is caused by the fact that many men and women are not content to be the sort of beings that God has made them, but try to persuade themselves that they are really beings of some different kind. They may act upon the assumption that they are simply a superior grade of mammal and that their spiritual powers and aspirations are a mere epiphenomenon of an organism essentially describable in terms of biology and nothing more. They may, on the other hand, act upon the assumption that they are pure spirits temporarily equipped with a physical organism which may be viewed as either a nuisance or a tool or a plaything but is in any case something that the human being *has*, not part of what he *is*. Whichever of these hypotheses they adopt is a false hypothesis and so is almost inevitably bound to issue in disas-

ter. Living like a gorilla is a very good thing to do if you
are a gorilla, and living like an angel is a very good thing
to do if you are an angel. And neither of these tasks is very
difficult for the being in question. If, however, you are a
human being you can achieve true happiness only by living
as a human being, and that is a much more difficult task. It
is, however, a task which has great compensations, and to
be a human being is to be a being who has a unique and
extremely exciting status in the universe; for it is to be a
dweller in both the great realms of creation, the realm of
matter and the realm of spirit.

The scriptural exegete may dispute whether the text from
the Epistle to the Hebrews from which I have already quoted,
and which ultimately derives from the eighth psalm, asserted
in its original context that man has been made a little lower
than the angels, or a little lower than God, or lower than the
angels for a little time, but in fact all three interpretations
seem to be theologically true: first, man's dual nature, composed of matter and spirit, although it places him below the
summit of creation, places him at its centre and this is a
very good place to be; second, man as a rational being bears
upon himself the stamp of the image of God; third, the fact
that his nature has been assumed by the Second Person of
the Blessed Trinity has raised it to a dignity that even angelic
nature has not known. There is certainly nothing that anyone need be ashamed of in being a human being, but it is a
task that calls for diligence, humility and, in view of our
fallen condition, for the grace of God. This last will be
considered later on.

There are many other puzzling characteristics of human
experience which become intelligible if we take with full

seriousness the dual nature of man. For example, there is
no reason for dismay in the fact that even our highest and
most spiritual activities depend for their exercise upon the
proper functioning of our bodies, that we can, to take two
concrete instances, neither philosophise clearly nor pray
attentively if we are suffering from influenza or arthritis or
from some disorder of the ductless glands. For it is the whole
human being as a psycho-physical entity that philosophises
or prays, and not merely his spirit, even though it is in virtue of his spirituality that he is able to do it. Furthermore,
we can understand the peculiarly fallible and discursive character of human knowledge and reasoning, since it is as spiritual beings that we are able to indulge in reflective thought
at all, while our corporeality imposes on even our most
abstract thinking an apparatus of sensory imagery and a
technique of comparison and contrast. In Thomist terms,
mens convertit se ad phantasmata and we reason *per com-
positionem et divisionem*.

All our experience, in fact, takes upon itself this double
character of spirituality and materiality, for we live in the
borderland where matter is raised to the level of spirit and
spirit immerses itself in matter. It is in fact the capacity of
man to transcend the physical realm of which he is part, to
stand, as it were, outside it and contemplate it from above,
which has traditionally provided the chief ground for the
argument that man's soul is not just an epiphenomenon of
his animal body but is a substantial spiritual entity in itself.
In view of the claims of certain cyberneticians to devise
physical models for such typically human activities as the
capacity to abstract universals from particulars we ought
perhaps to be cautious about building too much upon this,

even while we recognise that some of the claims of the cyberneticians seem to be exaggerated. What is more significant even than our capacity of reflection and abstraction is our ability, when we contemplate the finite world which our senses present to us, to form, however remotely and obscurely, the notion of a self-existent infinite Spirit upon whom the world of our experience depends. For in doing this we are not merely passing from the particularity of sensory experience to the generality and universality of intellectual abstraction—a transition which remains within the finite order—but are passing to an intellectual apprehension which transcends the finite order itself. In man, therefore, we see, incorporated in the material realm, a spiritual factor which, bearing upon itself the image of God, can recognise God as the archetype and imprinter of that image and can raise the material realm itself to the level of spirit. Man is thus on the frontier where matter impinges upon spirit and itself becomes spiritualised, not by losing its own materiality but by becoming one organism with the spirit which assumes it, that bipartite organism of body and soul which is called man.

What further capacities this involves in man, of being raised to a still higher level which by his own unaided efforts he cannot achieve, is a question to which we shall turn farther on. What we can as yet claim to have seen is that in man, the apparently anomalous and ridiculous being which we are, the featherless biped who stalks the earth dreaming fantastic dreams and seeking the fulfilment of preposterous desires, matter has reached the point at which, through its assumption by spirit, it has become conscious of itself, and not only of itself but also of the Spirit who made and preserves it.

III · INDIVIDUAL AND SOCIETY [1]

One truth at least should have emerged from the last
chapter: namely, that a human being is a very complicated
kind of thing. But more complication is to come. In the last
chapter we considered the complication which each human
being, as a unity of body and soul, has in himself. Now we
must pass on to consider the complication that comes from
man's situation in relation to his fellows, his relation as an
individual to society.

It is, I suppose, conceivable that God might have made
each man to be an entirely self-contained individual, incapsulated in a kind of impermeable membrane, solely concerned with his own interior life. Such a being might have
been something like a finite version of Aristotle's prime
mover, unconscious of the existence of anything but himself, engaged in pure self-contemplation, *noēsis noēseōs*. Or
he might have been made to be like one of Liebnitz' monads,
having an indirect knowledge of the world from which it
was cut off, because it had been provided with a divinely
authenticated news-film exhibited to it in the private theatre
of its own consciousness. On the other hand, it is also conceivable that God might have made each individual to be

nothing more than a cell in the organism of the human race, with no genuine consciousness and life of its own, enjoying in fact the same kind of existence that, according to some observers, seems to be enjoyed—if that is the word to use—by the individual members of a colony of ants. But in actuality God has made man in neither of these ways. Man is an individual and a member of the human community, and both these aspects are equally fundamental to his being. The institutions and conventions of society are not just tiresome but necessary compromises agreed upon by aggregates of self-asserting individualists in order to allow each to achieve the maximum amount of self-assertion which is possible without his being inconvenienced by the self-assertiveness of others. They are the positive means through which a man can achieve a true life in community and can fully develop and express the sociality which is an essential characteristic of his nature. It is of course perfectly possible that in some human groupings the institutional and conventional element may be exaggerated, and that in others it may be underdeveloped; this does not affect the point at issue. It is this dual character of individuality and sociality that is implied when we describe the human being as a *person*.

The concept of personality is not, of course, confined to Christianity or even to the Judaeo-Christian revelation, but it is very significant that it was only when it entered into theology, through the controversies in the early Church about the nature of God, that its full content and implications became manifest. For Christianity believes both that men are persons and that God is three Persons in one essence. The complete mutual penetration of the divine Persons and the complete possession of the fullness of the Godhead by each provide the archetype of the real but partial mutual penetration of human beings and their real but relative possession of human nature as members of the human race. The idea of personality was present in Greek thought only in embryo, and to this day it is practically absent from Hinduism and Buddhism.

Our first business, then, is to elucidate the notion of personality. An obvious starting-point is the classical definition given by Boethius that a person is an individual substance of a rational nature.[2] Dryly scholastic as these words may sound, there is implicit in them all the splendour of St. Thomas' declaration that of all things in nature a person is the most perfect: [3] *substance* expresses a man's permanence and self-identity; *individual* his real unity; and *rational* his dignity as an intelligent being, made in the image of the God who is Truth. But the most illuminating discussion of the meaning of personality that I can remember having seen is that which was given nearly twenty years ago by Jacques Maritain, in his essay on "The Human Person and Society," [4] and it is this to which I shall now refer.

Maritain begins by making a very important distinction between personality and individuality, though each of these, as he points out, belongs to every man. Whereas individuality is common to him and all other corporeal beings, personality belongs, among corporeal beings, to man alone. Individuality is what marks a man as distinct from every other being, as *this* in contrast to *that*, as *I* in contrast to *those*; it is rooted in the material side of man's nature, in his body. It is indeed a great mystery, but personality is an even greater one; it is rooted in his spiritual element, in his soul; and it is best approached by a consideration of love. For love, which is essentially self-giving, is focused not upon anything that the loved one possesses—not upon qualities, natures, or essences—but upon the person that he or she *is*. In Maritain's own words:

In order to be able to *give oneself*, one must first exist, and not only as the sound which passes in the air, or this idea which crosses my mind, but as a thing which subsists and which by itself exercises existence. And one must not only exist as other things, one must exist in an eminent way, by possessing oneself, by holding oneself in hand and by disposing of oneself; that is, one must exist through a spiritual existence, capable of enveloping itself by intelligence and freedom, and of *super-existing* in knowledge and free love. That is why the Western metaphysical tradition defines the person by independence: the person is a reality, which, subsisting spiritually, constitutes a universe by itself and an independent whole (relatively independent), in the great whole of the universe and facing the transcendent Whole, which is God. And that is why this philosophical tradition sees in God the sovereign personality, since God's existence consists in a pure and absolute super-existence of intellection and love.[5]

God, then, is supremely personal because he is the supreme reality. And because we are persons—and in the fullness of our personal existence express ourselves to ourselves—we seek to communicate ourselves to others.

Moral development consists in becoming, through the action of our own wills, that which in essence and principle we already are. And there are two directions of movement between which the will can choose. There is the line of individuality, of the material, which will lead a man to suck into himself from his environment all that he can, thus becoming the "hateful ego"; and there is the line of personality, of the spiritual, in which he will find his full self-realisation and perfection by giving himself to others, thus treading in the path of the saints. And because personality involves this activity of self-giving, it is essentially social. As Vladimir Soloviev says, " 'this' can become 'all' only in company with 'others.' " [6] In Maritain's words, "it is essential for personality to tend towards communion." [7] Aristotle, Maritain asserts, was quite right in saying that man is naturally a political animal; the end of society is its common good, the common good of the body politic. Yet this common good is a good of human persons, and this is what the totalitarian systems have denied. Man as an *individual* is indeed subordinate to society, as the part is subject to the whole. Nevertheless, because man is a *person*, society—being composed of persons—is a "whole of wholes." Through the fact of personality, "a single human soul is of more worth than the whole universe of bodies and material goods. There is nothing above the human soul—except God. In regard to the eternal destiny of the soul and its supra-temporal goods, society exists for each person and is subordinated to it." [8]

Thus, since the person as such is a whole and the individual as such is a part, human society inevitably involves a state of tension and conflict. This is in the nature of things, and the solution is not static but dynamic. There is a twofold movement: a horizontal one, whereby the person enters into a life of mutual self-giving with the other persons who form human society, and a vertical one, whereby the person, in his concrete possession of himself, transcends his status as a mere member of the community, as just one unit among others. Thus, by the very law of his being, because of the odd sort of creature that he is, the human person both requires society and rises above it.

One need not go all the way with Maritain's strict Thomist Aristotelianism in order to accept the general features of his exposition. There are, however, some important comments that we can add.

The doctrine of personality invests the human being with a most bracing, and at the same time a terrifying, combination of dignity and lowliness. As a person, man is subject to nothing but God; he is "the most perfect thing in all nature," and God has "put all things under his feet." But he *is* subject to God, and he does belong to the natural order. Hence, his full potentialities can be realised only by a humble acceptance of his condition as a creature and of the particular nature that God has given him. He must be ready to live, not as a disembodied spirit, but as the kind of being, composed of spirit and matter, that he actually is, in a right relationship to God, to his fellow men, and to the material earth which is the basis of his physical life.

Again, from what has been said, it will be clear that two of the noblest characteristics that personality involves are the capacity to make free and responsible decisions, and the capacity to give oneself in them. The rationality in which personality formally consists confers both the power and the duty to make decisions and to abide by their consequences; as God's vicegerent, bearing on himself the seal of God's image, man has been given a kind of finite and relative participation in the creative activity of God. And the sphere in which this freedom is supremely operative is that of his own inner life. It is because it holds this exalted conception of man, and not because it is callous to human suffering, that the great Christian tradition has maintained that a man can bind himself by irrevocable vows in marriage or the religious life, and has dared to insist on the awful doctrine of hell. As Eric Gill once wrote, the fact of hell "implies the most stupendous compliment to man conceivable," [9] for it means that God respects man's freedom to the point of allowing him to choose his own ultimate destiny. When the last word has been said about prevenient and subsequent, about sufficient and efficacious, grace, the fact remains that grace does not remove but instead intensifies man's freedom in his own acts. And it is to the point to notice that most of the ethical doctrines and denials put forward today as emancipating man from the trammels of a superstitious and priest-ridden age are concerned in one way or another with limiting his freedom or his fecundity. Maritain writes:

Man has achieved a fictitious emancipation, the waste and dispersal of the human substance in the endless multiplication of needs and sadness; the control of procreation not by chastity, but by doing violence to natural finalities; the control of the race by the eugenic sterilisation of defectives; the control of the self by the abolition of family ties and unconcern for descendants; the control of life by liberty to commit suicide and euthanasia. It is remarkable that a certain conception of the control of nature by man is compensated in the balance sheet, with startling uniformity, by one single consequence: the cessation of life.[10]

From the emphasis that has been laid above upon the fact that one of the noblest characteristics of human personality is the power to *give oneself*, there is a natural transition to consideration of the family. For the family is set up by a complete and, as Christianity alleges, an irrevocable giving of two persons to each other for what theology calls *consortium totius vitae*, "the sharing of the whole of life," a giving whose permanent character is manifested by the fact

that the private offering and acceptance of the man and
woman by each other is expressed by a public interchange
of vows in the face of the social community or its repre-
sentatives, and which is ultimately sealed by a physical act
which is of so intimate a nature and penetrates so deeply
into every recess, both physical and mental, of the personality
that, according to traditional Christian doctrine, nothing
within the order of nature, except the death of one of the
parties, can subsequently relax the union that has been set
up between them. Indeed, it would appear that even death
does not, strictly speaking, *break* the union, although by
removing from it the possibility of physical expression, it
makes a subsequent union on the part of the surviving part-
ner possible. (Even so, it must be noted that the Church has
not been altogether comfortable about second marriages.)
And the effect of this mutual self-giving of person to person
is to set up a new social unity composed of them both, whose
name is the family and whose existence is based not merely
on a contract, which might conceivably be voided by mutual consent or unilateral violation, but upon a real and
objective act by which the two persons have, in a sense
which is not merely metaphorical, *become one*. They are,
in the biblical phrase, "one flesh." [11] Hence, as Christian
tradition teaches, indissolubility is not confined to Christian
marriage, but is rooted in marriage as a natural human institution.

It should be clear from this how far removed the Christian
doctrine of marriage is from the elaborate system of repres-
sion, designed to prevent any positive or thoroughgoing
operation of the instinct of sex, which the lamentably bourgeois mentality of many of its exponents has often made it

seem to be. On the contrary, the insistence of Christian tradition upon irrevocability and finality means that there are some things that a human being can do so positively and whole-heartedly that he can never go back on them, since in them he has made a gift, not of anything belonging to him nor even of a part of him, but of his whole and very self in its concrete totality. It is the various non-Christian attitudes to sex that are half-hearted, anaemic, and invertebrate, for they claim for man the right to follow his impulses without taking the responsibility for his decisions and accepting the consequences of his actions. They are thus essentially infantile. Maurice Reckitt has well written:

The defence of Christian marriage is not only the safeguarding of an institution. . . . It is the vindication of the romantic and the heroic in man. . . . If "limited liability" is the true outlook on marriage, then not only is Christian doctrine false, but half the poetry and romance of the world are thereby declared to be meaningless. . . . That love should lack faith in its own permanence and the courage to pledge itself in vows is the sign not of a vital and full-blooded generation, but of a spiritless and enfeebled one.[12]

And it is impossible not to be struck by the amount of anxiety that is raised and of energy that is wasted in the task of "keeping your husband (or wife) faithful to you" among those for whom marriage relies for stability not upon something objective and irrevocable that has happened once and for all, but merely upon the personal attractiveness that each party can continue to exercise on the other as the years go on.

There are, it must be repeated, certain decisions that so completely implicate a man in the totality of his being that they are irreversible; and of none can this be more obviously true than of marriage. Husband and wife literally "throw themselves away" on each other. The plain fact is that it is impossible to live life to the full unless one is prepared for the tremendous consequences that human personality involves. The condemnation under which the "new moralities" fall from the Christian standpoint is not that they are too full-blooded but that they are sterile. As C. S. Lewis has said, "it would seem that our Lord finds our desires, not too strong, but too weak. We are half-hearted creatures, fooling about with drink and sex and ambition when infinite joy is offered us. . . . We are far too easily pleased." [13]

It was asserted above that the new social unity which is called the family is set up by the mutual union of husband and wife; no mention was made of children. This is in line with the general Catholic teaching, which has never treated sterility or voluntary abstinence as making a marriage null, while impotence (that is, powerlessness to complete the mutual union) is accepted as a ground for nullity. And in recent years theologians have tended strongly to the view that the mutual perfection of husband and wife is the primary reason of marriage. Père Emile Mersch, Herbert Doms, Dietrich von Hildebrand, the pseudonymous T. G. Wayne, and, in my own communion, G. Bryan Bentley can all be quoted for this view. [14] And if the present pope has approved a decree of the Holy Office condemning the view, [15] his predecessor, in his famous encyclical on Christian marriage, explicitly taught it. [16] It is this view, rather than any view of procreation as the supreme end of marriage, that provides, in my judgement, the most convincing argument yet urged against artificial contraception; it can be found in Doms's excellent work *The Meaning of Marriage*.[17] Nevertheless, it is a fact that the union of man and woman is also the act, and the only natural act (for nothing could be more unnatural than artificial insemination), through which the production of new members of the human race is mediated. There is no *a priori* reason for this: it is possible to imagine rational beings in whom the two functions were quite disconnected, and for all we know such may exist in some distant part of the universe. As Doms remarks:

Animals reproduce in a great number of typically different ways. The all-powerful God, who made man both physical and spiritual and, as far as his body is concerned, very like some animals, could have made him reproduce in any one of these ways. Or he could have invented for man's use a totally new means of generation. . . . He chose to make man be born the offspring not of one but of two parents. He chose to make him a feeble creature, at first absolutely dependent on others and doomed to grow for a score of years before becoming fit to go through life alone.[18]

It follows that, while husband and wife together may form a perfectly genuine human family, the normal result of their union will be the procreation of children, and the purpose of the marriage relationship will then be widened to include the mutual sanctification not of the parents alone but of parents and children together as one community. And, even if the essential *meaning* of marriage is the mutual union of husband and wife, the procreative end is one of transcendent splendour and dignity. For it witnesses to an almost incredible gift of God to man, namely the power to co-operate with God in the production of new human persons, before whom lies the vocation to eternal life in the beatific vision of God in heaven.[19] "The replenishing first of earth with blessed inhabitants and then of heaven with saints everlastingly praising God did depend upon conjunction of man and woman," wrote the great Anglican theologian Richard Hooker.[20] Jeremy Taylor remarks even more succinctly that "marriage is the nursery of heaven." [21] The precept of Genesis, "Be fruitful and multiply," [22] is not an arbitrary command externally imposed but is the expression of a constitutive characteristic of human nature. For these reasons perhaps the most adequate definition of the end of marriage would be given by saying that it is for the increase of the population of heaven, and that within this end there may be distinguished the two intimately interlocked goods which theology describes as *bonum fidei* (upon which is based the *consortium totius vitae*) and *bonum prolis:* in plain English, fidelity and fertility, faithfulness and fruitfulness.

To avoid all ambiguity it will be well to state plainly that what I have been expounding is not the Christian doctrine about Christian marriage, but the Christian doctrine about marriage as a natural human institution; in specifically Christian marriage there is, beside the two goods mentioned above, the *bonum sacramenti,* by which the whole complex of relationships that go to make up marriage is lifted up from the natural to the supernatural level, in virtue of which, as St. Paul told the Ephesians,[23] marriage is analogous to, and is subsumed into, the union between Christ and the Church.

Since, as we have seen, the family as an institution rests upon the mutual self-giving of two persons, its position in relation to the community is similar to that of the person itself. Even on the purely biological plane it has a certain priority to the community, for it is rooted in the biological fact of mammalian reproduction. It is, however, far more than biological in its essence; it is personal, a unity of persons, involving every level of their being from matter up to spirit. Hence, although the family—like the individual—is in a certain sense subordinate to the community because the community as a whole includes families among its parts, there is a far more important sense in which the community is subordinate to the family: the community is a society of persons whom it links together by relations, many of which are beneath the personal level, while the family is a consequence of the highest activity of which persons are capable in the natural order. Any system of planning that tends to disrupt rather than to safeguard the family is therefore to be condemned, as much from the purely natural as from the specifically religious point of view; and, just as one criterion by which to judge planning is its probable effect upon persons, so another criterion is its probable effect upon families. It should be added that in a disordered society the family, if it manages to resist disintegration at all, tends to become introverted and exclusive, and even predatory and parasitic, in sheer self-defence, and, instead of making a living and spontaneous contribution to the life of the community as a whole, it encloses itself in a hard shell and becomes destructive of social solidarity. Then the state can easily come to look upon the family as an obstacle to social coherence and progress and can, in consequence, be led to increase that very pressure on the family which was the original cause of the trouble. Few tasks are more necessary in the social sphere than the establishment of the right balance between the state and the family.

Thus, whether we consider social relationships in general or the particular and basic relationship of marriage and the family, we see in man, as God has made him, an essential *openness* towards his fellows, which implies that his personality can develop freely and fully only in community. It needs, however, to be emphasised that a community itself, whether the community of the family or of some other group, can develop freely and fully only if its activity transcends a mere concern of the members with one another and issues in outgoing, constructive activity. Lovers must not for ever be gazing in each other's eyes. It is in common activity that man realises not only his community with other men but also his organic relationship with the world as a whole—the world of matter of which he himself is a part because he is body as well as soul, and of which, as God's vicegerent, stamped with God's image, he is the priest who by his wise and reverent manipulation and employment of the world is to make it a fit offering to the glory of its Creator. Never in the course of human history has the recognition of this truth been as important as it is today, when man has acquired a power over the material creation which, whether for good or for evil, involves the most gigantic and terrifying possibilities. As Etienne Borne and François Henry wrote, in their book *A Philosophy of Work:*

It seems possible [I would say "It seems certain"] that souls are not created directly for one another, but that they need to be gathered together before they can be united; they must recognise one another in a visible activity, before they can know one another in complete intimacy. This means that a spontaneous impulse of the affections is not sufficient to constitute a friendship. For the creation of such a close relationship there must exist what Maurice Blundel calls by the happy name of the Heteronomy of Creative Work.[24]

These authors have indeed drastic judgements to pass upon the servile notion of work which has become characteristic of the modern world, a world which has grown up under the domination of a conception of life in financial and mercantile terms, a world in which, in a famous pontifical phrase, matter leaves the factory ennobled but men leave it degraded. And it is well to remember that men can be degraded as much by prosperity as by privation if their scale of values is distorted or inverted. But of work itself, as a human activity, Borne and Henry cannot speak too highly. There exists no better preparation than work, they say, for the life of contemplation.[25] And again:

The six days of labour are a preparation for the divine repose of the seventh day. Also it is from the repose of the seventh day that labour emerges both more fruitful and more fraternal. The harmonious city would be that in which work is not the foe of contemplation, but in which effort should temper souls capable of enduring the terrible and holy energy of God himself, and in which the souls freighted with love by their intimate conversation with God should go out to spread abroad that love widely and superabundantly in labour, having no avarice, but in a saintly prodigality, because they know full well that the best means of saving love is to spend it without counting the cost.[26]

There are, of course, in any society jobs to be done which are tedious or distasteful, and the problem of organising them in such a way as to avoid the exploitation of the unfortunate by the prosperous and the degradation of those who do them is a highly complex one which I can make no attempt to solve in detail here. I would, however, suggest that one of the signs of a healthy society is that the distinction between

work and play does not coincide with the distinction between the unpleasant and the pleasant. In Eric Gill's words:

> The free man does what he likes in his working time
>   and in his spare time what is required of him.
> The slave does what he is obliged to do in his working time
>   and what he likes to do only when he is not at work.[27]

But to return to our former point, it is the contemplation
of God in prayer that must be both the source and the end
of all human activity in society. The astounding energy
which has marked the lives of many of the great contem-
plative saints will no longer seem paradoxical or unexpected
if we recall that in their prayer they are energised by the
God who is pure and absolute energy, and that their activity
is an overflow from their prayer, that it proceeds *ex super-
abundantia contemplationis*. And if contemplation is the
source of all fruitful and rightly co-ordinated activity, it is
also the ultimate end to which that activity is directed. For
the end for which each man is made is the contemplation of
God in heaven. This is a contemplation to be enjoyed by
each man not as an isolated individual soul but as a fully
integrated human being and a member of the Body of Christ.
The Christian proclaims his belief in the communion of
saints, the resurrection of the body, and the life everlasting.
We may leave the last word on the matter with the Angelic
Doctor:

> Sufficiency of corporal goods and of the life of virtue is the end
> of human confederation; but since the life of virtue is itself or-
> dained to something infinitely higher—namely, the blessed vision
> of God—the ultimate purpose of individual human life must be
> also the ultimate purpose of any human confederation.
> The end of the State is therefore the vision of God.[28]

IV · NATURE AND SUPERNATURE

As we saw in the second chapter, according to one interpretation of the Biblical text man has been made a little lower than the angels: although his dual nature, composed of matter and spirit, places him below the summit of creation, it places him at the centre; and this, I wrote, was a very good place in which to be. He lives on the frontier where the two regions of matter and spirit impinge on each other; or, to speak more accurately, in him the two regions of matter and spirit overlap. As a creature, however, he lives upon a more interesting frontier still, the frontier where the Creator impinges upon his creation. Can we go further than this and find some sense in which we can legitimately say that in man the created and the uncreated not only impinge upon each other but also overlap? According to a different but equally legitimate interpretation of the text, man has been made a little lower than God himself; as a rational creature he bears upon himself the stamp of the image of God. How are such expressions as this to be understood? And what does the Second Epistle of St. Peter mean when it declares that we may become partakers of the divine nature? [1] What, in short, is involved in the fact that man is a rational creature? This is the question to which we must now turn.

First of all, a rational creature is a creature, and creaturehood itself is, from the point of view of Christian theism, a
remarkably delicate and paradoxical status. For ancient Greek
thought, as for eighteenth-century deism, every being has a
nicely rounded-off nature which contains implicitly all it
can ever become; if we only knew that nature properly we
should know all that it ever could be. Even ancient Greeks
had to admit that in actual practice things do not work out
quite as neatly as this; there is, they said, both in ourselves
and in the world around us, a tiresome factor called matter
which makes things largely unintelligible and our knowledge of them very obscure. If we want to achieve exhaustive
understanding of completely transparent realities we must
abandon everyday life and physical science for contemplation of the perfect ideas of pure mathematics. This is trouble-
some and embarrassing, but the fundamental point was unchanged, namely, that in so far as a thing is intelligible at
all, its intelligibility is implicit in its form. In whatever way
we suppose things derive their existence, all they can ever
become is given them at the start. If a being changes in some
way, this can only be either because its form is being more
fully actualised, as when a child becomes a man; or because,
in consequence of its material component, it is suffering
decay, as when a man becomes senile; or because its nature
is being changed into a different nature altogether, as when
a man's food is absorbed into his body. The one thing that is
impossible—impossible because from the Greek standpoint it
is strictly unintelligible—is that a nature should increase in
perfection by acquiring some characteristic which was not
implicit in it from the beginning. Owing to the obscurity
which matter introduces into the world, we generally have

to be content with nominal definitions of things in place of essential definitions; but if we once knew the essential definition of a thing we should know in principle everything there was to know about it. All that it was and all that it ever could be would be given to us in the definition, in the same way as all the properties of a triangle follow from the definition of the triangle. For once you know what a thing is, what else can there be to know about it? Such was the Greek view.

Now, as we saw when we were considering Josef Pieper's comments on Sartre, Christian theology is very much concerned to maintain that things have natures, but its view of what natures are and why things have them is totally different from that of ancient Greece. For the pagan Platonist, a number of rabbits looked more or less alike and behaved in more or less the same way because they were numerically different and variously imperfect embodiments of the ideal rabbit which lay up in heaven while these sported in the fields. For the Christian, they look and behave alike because God has made them in the same way. Whatever views Christian philosophers have adopted about the relation between universals and particulars—and the history of medieval philosophy bears sufficient witness to the diversity of those views—they have agreed that the only place where the ideas of things exist, except in the things themselves, is in the mind of God. It was the brilliant achievement of St. Thomas Aquinas to combine with his Christianised Aristotelianism a Christianised Platonism, for which things exist not because they reflect or embody the forms of a static and spectral realm of ideas, but because they are creatively thought by God. Etienne Gilson has eloquently shown what this transformation meant to Christian metaphysics,[2] for Christian metaphysics has a clear grasp of the fact that the ultimate question about finite beings is not why they are the sort of beings that they are, but why they exist at all. And the answer which Christian theism gives to that question is that they exist simply and entirely because they are being incessantly created, conserved, and energised by God, because they are radically and totally dependent upon the creative activity of a Being who is entirely perfect and self-existent.

This does not mean that finite beings are lacking in reality; on the contrary, they have all the reality that finite beings can have. They are real but dependent beings, exercising real but dependent energies; they have nothing that they have not received, but they have not received nothing. Nor does this mean that they have no genuine community of nature with one another. On the contrary, when God creatively thinks two beings in the same way, this constitutes a common nature for them. As Pieper shows, Christian theism safeguards and does not deny the reality of finite essences. As I have said elsewhere:

Although it is true that, if God ceased to conserve a creature it would cease to exist, the fundamental truth is that so long as God conserves it it goes on existing, and exists with all those energies and perfections which he communicates to it. Nevertheless, the mere fact that it is not self-existent means that it is not ontologically incapsulated in itself; to be a finite being is to be essentially *open*, open to the activity of God, who, without annulling or withdrawing anything that he has given, can always give more.[3]

And in man, who, as a rational being, bears in himself the seal of God's own image, this openness involves the most amazing possibilities. It provides the basis for that whole complex of theological doctrine which is associated with the words "grace," "supernature," and "deification" in Catholic ascetics.

The traditional way of stating the matter in the Catholic text-books is to distinguish sharply between a natural condition of man, which is proper to him simply in virtue of his rational nature, and a supernatural condition, to which he cannot attain by the exercise of his own powers but to which he can be raised by the purely gratuitous act of God. Corresponding to these there is alleged to be, first, a purely natural knowledge of God as the Creator of all things, which can in principle lead to the exercise of purely natural virtues and a purely natural beatitude, and, second, a supernatural knowledge of God, which is the direct result of supernatural grace, is correlative with the supernatural virtue of charity, and culminates in the supernatural beatitude of the vision of God in heaven. It is added that, in the fallen condition in which he finds himself, man needs the grace of God even to achieve an undistorted knowledge of God as the Creator and to practice the natural virtues; fallen man needs not only *gratia elevans* but *gratia sanans* as well. Nevertheless, we are told, there is a clear distinction to be drawn between, on the one hand, a natural knowledge of God and a natural beatitude, which are proper to man the rational creature as the highest denizen of the material universe and which are in principle attainable by his normal natural powers; and, on the other hand, a supernatural knowledge of God and a supernatural beatitude, which man by his nature can neither expect nor claim and which is a pure, unconditioned gift from God. Man's nature has indeed a capacity to receive this gift, for it is a gift which is possible only to a rational being.

Human nature is capable of deification, equine nature is not; but this capacity is, to use the technical phrase, a *potentia oboedientialis*, a capacity of sheer passive reception, and man would be in no way incomplete or frustrated if it were left unactualised.

The difficulties in this position are well known. It appears to make supernature into a mere superstructure, like an extra storey put on an already complete building as an afterthought, having no organic relationship with the substructure of nature which supports it. Furthermore, it appears to make man's supreme beatitude, the vision of God, into a kind of optional appendage which might hardly seem worth striving for if beatitude can be achieved without it. Again, Catholic theology itself has been forced to recognise that man has a natural desire for the vision of God, although it insists that man has no right to claim it and no natural power to achieve it. To reconcile this with the accepted principle that it is impossible for a natural desire to be unsatisfied has strained the ingenuity of scholastic theologians to the breaking point.

A large amount of Catholic writing has been devoted in recent years to various aspects of this problem, as, for example, J. E. O'Mahony's book, *The Desire of God in the Philosophy of St. Thomas Aquinas;* Patrick Bastable's *Desire for God;* and Père Henri de Lubac's valuable historical study, *Surnaturel.* I cannot attempt here to give an account of this debate. I shall only ask the question whether, along with a great many Protestant critics, we must reject altogether this distinction between the natural and the supernatural and with it the whole notion of man's deification, his elevation into the life of God. My answer will be that we need not.

We must indeed freely admit that many of the Catholic manualists have conceived the relation between nature and supernature in far too rigid and superficial a manner. I do not mean by this that I think the distinction between nature and supernature is mistaken; on the contrary, I think it is quite vital. But it has often been used in a way which is suggestive of the Greek doctrine of a nature as a rounded and sealed entity, rather than of the Christian doctrine which sees it as perpetually dependent upon and open to the creative activity of God. In consequence, the sole function which nature appears to perform for supernature is that of providing a kind of platform upon which the latter is built. Indeed, the two orders seem sometimes to be conceived as so devoid of any organic interrelation that it becomes difficult to see why, if human nature has a *potentia oboedientialis* for supernature only in this minimal sense, equine or scarabeic nature should not have it too. On the other hand, it needs to be recognised that Reformation Protestant theology's common denial that grace can bring about any real transformation of human nature seems to rest upon a very similar assumption that human nature is something essentially closed. I do not suggest that there has been a direct influence of pagan Greek thought upon either the Catholic manualists or the Protestant theologians. It seems much more probable that the real cause in both cases is an uncriticised inheritance from the nominalist metaphysics of the late Middle Ages, which was simply incapable of conceiving any real changes in a being which were not empirically verifiable.[4]

Be this as it may, I suggest that most of the difficulties in
the Catholic doctrine of nature and supernature disappear if
we remember the essentially open character of all finite
beings. At first sight it may seem shocking to say that, without any defect in his love, God might have refrained from
conferring upon his creature some gift which it was in his
power to bestow—that, for example, God might have given
man no more than a purely natural beatitude. The scandal
will, however, be lessened when we reflect that, however
great may be the gifts which God actually confers upon his
creature, he might always have conferred greater, and this
not because there is any failure in his power or his love but
simply because there is no maximum finite quantity; because,
given *any* finite quantity, however great, there are an infinite number of finite quantities which are greater. Even in
the beatific vision, wherein man sees God himself, man sees
God in the finite way which is possible to him; *totum sed
non totaliter*, as the schoolmen say.[5] "God, whose being is
infinite," writes St. Thomas, "is infinitely knowable." Nevertheless, "since the created light of glory received into any
created intellect cannot be infinite, it is impossible for any
created intellect to know God in an infinite degree. . . .
The created intellect knows the divine essence more or less
perfectly in proportion as it receives a greater or lesser light
of glory." [6] There are in fact two things that we must remember about God's gifts to us. The first is that whatever
God has given to us is more than we had any right to demand. The second is that, whatever God has given us, it is
always in his power to give us more. The attitude of the
Christian before God should thus combine gratitude and
contentment with expectancy and wonder; and it is diffi-

cult to conceive of anything more exhilarating than this. The Christian life is in fact one of constant surprises; the Christian quite literally never knows what is coming next. "Of his fulness we have all received," writes St. John, "and one grace after another" (*charin anti charitos*).[7]

The fundamental openness of man's being to God's activity is thus the metaphysical basis of the Catholic doctrine of the elevation of man's nature to the level of supernature by grace. And just as nature itself can be supernaturalised, so supernaturalised nature is capable of further supernaturalisation. It is quite wrong to think simply of two levels, one being the level of nature and the other the level of supernature. If we are going to use the image of levels at all, we should think of an infinite sequence of levels, each in contact with those below and above. But indeed the imagery of levels, while it has its uses, is quite inadequate, for it fails to do justice to the intimacy of the relation between them. There are two Thomist tags, one very well known, the other less so, which add what is lacking to this formulation. "Grace perfects nature and does not destroy it," [8] the Angelic Doctor tells us, but also "grace presupposes nature." [9] It is quite wrong to suppose that grace is a kind of supernatural substance and that nature exists for the sake of it. On the contrary, grace apart from nature is a pure abstraction; and it is for the sake of nature that grace exists. Supernature simply means nature supernaturalised by grace, and the possibility of this supernaturalisation lies in the openness of nature to God. For a nature which was closed in the Greek sense, supernaturalisation would be identical with destruction, for it could only mean the replacement of one nature by another. But for a nature which is open in the Christian sense, supernaturalisation means expansion, development, perfection, a realisation of hitherto unsuspected potentialities, a new infusion of the creative activity of God; and when this supernaturalisation has taken place unlimited possibilities of further supernaturalisation lie ahead. In each stage of the process God takes the initiative; the creature can neither envisage what the next stage will be, nor demand its fulfilment as a right, nor initiate its achievement. Nevertheless, as the process goes on the creature finds its own activity not by-passed or suppressed, but on the contrary liberated and enhanced. The more it is supernaturalised, the more truly natural it becomes. And all this because openness to God is of its very essence; dependence upon him is part of its definition.

At this point it will be well to stress that it is the whole of man's nature, and not merely part of it, that is supernaturalised by grace. We saw in the second chapter how firm the Christian faith is upon the fact that the body is an integral part of human nature, so that a man is not to be simply identified with his soul. Practical religion, however, does not always come up to the level of Christian dogma, and, especially since the days of Descartes, the tendency to identify man with his soul for religious purposes has sometimes been very strong. It almost invariably goes hand in hand with a misunderstanding of the relation between nature and supernature and of the relation between the secular and the religious aspects of life. When the true balance is lost, the tendency invariably arises to identify nature with the body and supernature with the soul; religion becomes a purely spiritual concern, and matter is relegated to the secular realm. Thus, instead of the constructive and invigorating recognition that the whole of man's nature, body no less than soul, and the whole of his life, the secular aspect no less than the religious, are to be supernaturalised, we get only too often a narrow and introverted restriction of supernature to the realm of the religious and the spiritual, and an abandonment of the secular and the material to the purely natural realm. The consequences are grave, to soul as well as to body, and to the religious as well as to the secular aspect of life.

For the truth is that the three dualities with which we are concerned—the body and the soul, the secular and the religious, the natural and the supernatural—so far from being identical or coextensive, are radically distinct. The body-soul duality is not the same as the secular-religious duality, as is seen from the fact that body and soul together are concerned both with secular affairs and with religion. The secular-religious duality is not the same as the natural-supernatural duality, as is seen from the fact that there is such a thing as natural religion. Still less is the body-soul duality to be identified with the natural-supernatural, for, as I have been at pains to emphasise, the whole of human nature as psycho-physical, spiritual-and-material, soul-and-body unity is to be caught up to the supernatural level.

So much for the question of the relation between the natural and the supernatural order. Something must now be said about the nature of the supernatural as such. What is this supernaturalisation of nature about which so much has been said? What precisely happens to a human being when it is transformed by *gratia elevans*, when grace perfects it without destroying it?

Christian tradition, in East and West alike, has found only one word adequate to denote it—the word "deification." "God wishes to make you a god," writes St. Augustine, "not

by nature but by adoption. Thus the whole man is deified." [10]
And in this he is only echoing the Second Epistle of St.
Peter, with its assertion that "you may become partakers of
the divine nature." The use of such phrases as these may
indeed seem astounding, for one of the truths upon which
the Christian Church, with its ancestry in Jewish monothe-
ism, has been most insistent is that the distinction between
God and even the highest of his creatures is absolute, that
no concessions can be made to any form of pantheism. And
Christian theologians, from the Fathers to the present day,
have been explicit that even at the heights of mystical union
with the Creator the creature does not lose his creaturely
status; the one thing that he cannot undergo is an entitative
transformation into the substance of God. Yet they have
been equally convinced that no term less than "deification"
is adequate to describe the condition of the human being
who has been taken by grace into the supernatural realm;
and, let us note, not simply the condition of the mystic
united to God in the spiritual marriage or of the saint enjoying the beatific vision in heaven, but also that of the newly
baptised infant at the font or of the newly absolved sinner
in the confessional.

Now, like most of the other realities with which Christian
theology deals, the condition with which we are here concerned is altogether unique. It follows, therefore, that any
attempt to describe it will suffer from all the limitations to
which analogical discourse in general is subject. Obviously,
I cannot attempt to give a reasoned argument here for the
possibility and propriety of analogical discourse; that must
be taken for granted. We will merely remind ourselves, as

we approach the task of description, of the drawbacks under which our speech inevitably labours.

First, then, the supernaturalisation which grace produces operates in the very substance of human nature, far beneath the level of observable behavior, even if it ultimately produces effects on the observable level. It may, and indeed it normally will, issue in the production of virtues, but they are its consequences and not its essence.

Second, while it works by transforming man's natural being, grace is directly concerned with his supernatural end and makes his natural end ancillary and contributary to it. That is to say, it orients him towards the vision of God and makes even the natural virtues helps to the achievement of that vision and not simply to the achievement of earthly happiness. The virtues which are its immediate effects are those supernatural virtues, of which the three theological virtues of faith, hope, and charity are typical, which are directly concerned with man's union with God; but under its overarching influence even the natural virtues—typified by the four cardinal virtues of justice, prudence, fortitude, and temperance—cease to be concerned simply with life in this world and contribute to the attainment of the beatific vision.

Third—and here we come to the point at which human language begins to fail—intimate as is the activity of God at the ontological root of our being, by which he keeps us in existence and energises our nature, far more intimate is his activity in us in the supernatural order. We might express the contrast by saying that in the natural order God gives us *our* selves, while in the supernatural order he gives us *his* self. Or we might say, with Père Emile Mersch: "The infinite Being has two ways of giving himself to finite beings; by the former, he gives himself to them in *their* way, which makes them themselves; by the latter he gives himself to them in *his* way, which makes them one with him." [11] Or again, we might say that in the natural order we live the finite life of a creature, while in the supernatural order we live the infinite life of God, even while we who live it are finite creatures and can therefore live it only in our finite way: *Quidquid recipitur reciptur ad modum recipientis.* If we are asked how so stupendous a thing should be possible, how it is conceivable that a creature can live with the life of the Creator, we can only point to the following truths. First, that finite beings are not sealed off from their Creator in a kind of impermeable capsule, but that their very existence depends upon God's incessant energising of them at the heart of their being. Second, that in man, the rational creature, finite being has reached a level at which it becomes conscious of its dependence upon God and thus can be not just a passive recipient of God's creative activity, but can, as it were, turn towards him and welcome him with open arms. This does not mean that man can achieve by his own efforts a new and higher kind of union with God, but it does mean that he can receive such a union if God wills to give it him, and that it will be not just the impersonal union of dependence which a created effect has with its uncreated cause, but a vital union of life and love between a personal creature and its personal Creator. In the nature of a rational being the created order reaches the apex at which, so to speak, it comes face to face with its Creator; as creature it is powerless to raise itself into the uncreated order, but as rational it is capable of enjoying the life of the uncreated order if God sees fit so to raise it.

The problems that this raises for our intellect are, it is needless to say, tremendous. I do not imagine that, given the Christian doctrine of creation and nothing more, anyone would have suspected that such a union as I have tried to describe was possible. Nevertheless, when we look back upon creation from the standpoint of revelation we can see that the one point at which such a union might conceivably take place would be the point at which a personal creature has become conscious of its dependence upon a personal God. At least we might dare to say that it would hardly make sense for God to confer such a union anywhere else. The mystery is that infinite being can be received in a finite mode. We might remind ourselves at this stage that the compresence of the finite and the infinite is always mysterious. At the very basis of Christian theism we are faced with the problem of why a self-sufficient God should create dependent beings; God's presence at the ontological root of all things as their Creator is mysterious enough in all conscience. Although God's union with man by grace is vastly more mysterious and wonderful than his presence in all his creatures by nature, I think we should be very insensitive if we began to feel intellectually baffled only when we came to consider grace and the supernatural. And it is God's presence in man as man's Creator that, together with man's rationality, provides the ground of man's *potentia oboedientialis* for elevation into the supernatural order.

There are three final points on which I shall briefly note in concluding this chapter.

First, it may well be asked why Protestantism has so firmly repudiated the notion that human nature is really transformed by grace and has limited the action of grace to a purely imputed righteousness that leaves human nature essentially unchanged. My answer is that Protestantism has done nothing of the sort, though official Protestant theology has. As Père Louis Bouyer has shown in his book *The Spirit and Forms of Protestantism*, Lutheranism and Calvinism have produced among their followers outstanding examples of men and women whose lives were transformed by sanctifying grace. And no one, I think, could have come into contact with sincere Lutherans and Calvinists today without being vividly conscious of the genuine holiness of their lives. In fact, one of the most striking characteristics of Protestantism when one meets it in its undiluted traditional forms is the violent contrast between its theology and its religion. The real question is why Protestant theology has been incapable of giving an adequate account of Protestant religion. And part at least of the answer to that question is provided by a fact to which I have previously drawn attention, namely the inheritance by Reformation theology of the nominalist thought forms of late medieval philosophy. For nominalism there can be no such thing as a supernatural transformation of a man's being in its ontological depths *beneath* the observable level, for on nominalist principles there is nothing beneath the observable level to transform. On the other hand, if grace were to produce a transformation *on* the observable level, the man would be justified by his own works, for on nominalist principles a man's observable behaviour is all that there is of him. Nothing, therefore, was left for Luther to say, since he was convinced that a man could not justify himself, except that there is no real change in the man at all, although, by imputing to him the merits of Christ, God treats him as if there was. It should be added that Catholic thinkers in the sixteenth century were as hamstrung as their Protestant opponents by the nominalist heritage; Père Bouyer has shown this clearly in the case of Erasmus.[12] And even when we go back to St. Thomas Aquinas we find the Angelic Doctor in great difficulties when he tries to give an account of the effect of grace upon the soul, though in his case it seems to me that his embarrassment comes not from any tendency to nominalism but from following too closely the naturalistic Aristotelian anthropology, with its assumption that human nature is basically rounded off and "closed." St. Thomas himself never adopts this assumption, but he has difficulty in shaking it off.

My second point is concerned with the rejection of the classical Western Catholic distinction between nature and supernature by the general theological tradition of Eastern Orthodoxy. The main features of that tradition have been made easily accessible by the recent translation into English of Vladimir Lossky's excellent book *The Mystical Theology of the Eastern Church*. Space does not allow a full discussion, but it is important to see how the conflict arises. The Eastern view, which is based upon the systematisation, by the fourteenth-century Archbishop of Thessalonica St. Gregory Palamas, of the doctrine of the fifth- or sixth-century writer Dionysius the pseudo-Areopagite, starts off from the position that God in his essence is absolutely unknowable and incommunicable. It compensates, however, for this "apophaticism" by making a distinction in God himself between his essence and his energies, and teaching that although he is incommunicable in essence, he is genuinely communicated in his energies. Criticising the Western outlook, Lossky writes:

Eastern tradition knows no such supernatural order between God and the created world, adding, as it were, to the latter a new creation. It recognises no distinction, or rather division, save that between the created and the uncreated. For Eastern tradition the created supernatural has no existence. That which Western theology calls by the name of the *supernatural* signifies for the East the *uncreated*—the divine energies ineffably distinct from the essence of God. The difference consists in the fact that the Western conception of grace implies the idea of causality, grace being represented as an effect of the divine Cause, exactly as in the act of creation; while for Eastern theology there is a natural procession, the energies, shining forth eternally from the divine essence. It is in creation alone that God acts as cause, in producing a new subject called to participate in the divine fulness; preserving it, saving it, *granting* grace to it, and guiding it towards its final goal.[13]

I must confess that I find the Palamite doctrine very difficult to follow and still more difficult to accept. But I doubt very much whether there is real *dogmatic* difference between East and West on this matter, sharply opposed as are the *theological* systems. If some Western theologians have meant by "the created supernatural" what Lossky thinks they have meant, I would agree with him against them. Any notion of the supernatural order as something which is neither God nor creature is, I suggest, avoided if one stresses, as I have stressed, the essentially *open* nature of the creature. Whatever difficulties are raised by the Western distinction between nature and supernature seem to me to be as nothing when compared with those that are raised by the Eastern distinction between the essence and the energies in God. However, in the matter with which we are concerned, the two distinctions seem in the long run to lead to much the same result; for each of them allows for a deification of man which does not destroy his creaturehood. One thing at least is clear, that the Eastern rejection of the Western Catholic doctrine of the supernatural has nothing in common with the Protestant rejection. For Eastern Orthodoxy places even more stress than Western Catholicism upon the deification of man. And there is a very "Western" ring about such sentences as the following, which occur in a passage in which the early sixth-century theologian Leontius of Byzantium expounds the contrast between the natural (*kata physin*), the unnatural (*para physin*), and the supernatural (*hyper physin*):

The act which is supernatural leads on and raises up [the natural] and empowers it for what is more perfect and to do those things which it could not do if it remained in the natural order. What is above nature does not destroy what is natural, but rather educes and stimulates it, both to be able to do the natural and to receive the power to do what is supernatural.[14]

Lastly, the question might be raised whether sub-rational creatures have any part in the supernaturalisation of nature. After all, it might be urged, their nature, no less than man's, is essentially open. The answer is, I suggest, that their part in the process of supernaturalisation is to participate in the life of deified man by ministering to his bodily needs. Their own nature cannot by itself be supernaturalized; for, while natural existence consists in the ontological dependence of a created effect upon its uncreated Cause, supernatural existence consists in an intercourse of life and love between a personal creature and its personal Creator. No sub-rational creature can *directly* participate in this. But if it ministers to the natural life of rational creatures it can participate in their supernaturalisation and so can be supernaturalised *mediately* and *indirectly*, and it is neither an exaggeration nor a joke to say that a cabbage or a sheep achieves its highest privilege in becoming the food of a Christian man. For man on his material side is directly involved in the natural order, while on his spiritual side he impinges upon the uncreated order of the divine life into which he can be elevated by grace. In his deification the whole order of nature is implicated through its ministerial relation to him; and in him as nature's priest it is itself offered to God and finds its place in the supernatural realm.

V · MAN FALLEN

If there are among my readers any whole-hearted adherents of the contemporary revival in Protestant Reformation theology, they will, I am sure, have already condemned me for substituting *analogia entis* for *analogia fidei* and *theologia gloriae* for *theologia crucis*. Four chapters about man's nature and his elevation by grace, and hardly a line about sin and redemption!

With all the genuine respect and admiration which I feel for the great modern movements in Protestant theology, it would be idle for me to pretend that I am in sympathy with them at all points, and one's sympathies are bound to affect the order in which one deals with one's subject. Still, if I cannot affirm with Jean-Jacques Rousseau that all my ideas are consistent, I can at least echo his plea that I cannot express them all at once.[1] And there seem to me to be great advantages in considering what man essentially is and what is the end for which God has made him, before turning one's attention to the sad condition in which we find him. And so in this chapter, whether belatedly or not, I shall think about man as fallen.

Even a cursory glance at the world around us or at our

own selves is sufficient to show that all is not well with man. When we go further, however, and inquire what exactly is wrong, who is to blame, and how, if at all, the wrong can be put right, we receive a baffling variety of answers. Hinduism and Buddhism will tell us that the trouble is due to our individual identity as separate persons in a differentiated world, and that to achieve beatitude we must either merge ourselves into the undifferentiated ocean of existence out of which we came, or turn our eyes inwards upon our own souls and seal ourselves off from all other beings, or cease to exist altogether and achieve a kind of ontological suicide. The dualistic systems, such as Zoroastrianism and Marcionism, have set a conflict at the very basis of being, either splitting God himself, as it were, into good and evil principles, or else frankly viewing God as malevolent or incompetent and offering us a saviour who will deliver us from him. However, in the modern world—and here it is not inappropriate to have mentioned the name of Rousseau—the predominant view, outside of strictly orthodox Christian circles has been that in spite of the misery in which most men have writhed and in spite of their gross exploitation by the privileged few, there is nothing really wrong that good will and enlightenment cannot correct; under the guidance of reason, judiciously tempered by revolution, man's steady progress to an earthly paradise is assured.

W. R. Thompson has remarked that "for the Victorian liberals, universal suffrage and universal education were passports to Utopia. They believed this because they thought of universal education as the power to attain Truth, and of universal suffrage as the ability to will Good."[2] Herbert

Butterfield has shown in his book *The Whig Interpretation of History* how a rationalist and progressist assumption distorted the work of some of the ablest historical scholars and led them to identify lateness in time with ethical excellence and to make the later the criterion by which the earlier was to be judged. But even by the beginning of this century the falsity of the assumption was beginning to be apparent. As long ago as 1904 G. K. Chesterton insisted: "There is a spirit abroad among the nations of the earth which drives men incessantly on to destroy what they cannot understand, and to capture what they cannot enjoy." [3] And Peter Drucker, writing during the Second World War, painted in striking colours the dilemma in which the political rationalist finds himself when he sees that things are not working out as he had expected:

He must maintain that his principles are rational, and that they can be made effective by rational means. He maintains as a dogma that his principles are rationally evident. Hence the rationalist liberal cannot attempt to translate them into political action except through rational conversion—which attempt must fail. On the one hand he cannot respect any opposition, for it can only be opposition to absolute truth. On the other hand, he cannot fight it. For error—and all opposition to his absolute truth must be error to a rationalist—can only be due to lack of information. . . .

On the one hand, the rationalist liberal cannot compromise. His is a perfectionist creed which allows of no concession. Anyone who refuses to see the light is an unmitigated blackguard with whom political relations are impossible. On the other hand, the rationalist cannot fight or suppress enemies. He cannot admit their existence. There can be only misjudged or misinformed people who, of necessity, will see reason when the incontrovertible evidence of the rational truth is presented to them. The rationalist

liberal is caught between holy wrath at conspirators and educa-
tional zeal for the misinformed. . . . He can neither compromise
for power nor fight for it. He is always paralysed politically.[4]

It is thus not surprising, as Drucker shows, that political
rationalism tends to degenerate into totalitarianism. For the
disillusioned rationalist can account for his failure only in
one of two ways. He may, on the one hand, reconcile his
belief in his theory with its failure in practice by postulat-
ing some gigantic hidden conspiracy which has thwarted and
perverted its natural consequences; there is a world-wide plot,
engineered by the Communists or the Freemasons or the Ro-
man Catholics or the Jews. Or, on the other hand—and this
is more likely if he is not himself psychologically unbalanced
—he may abandon his original assumption of man's per-
fectibility and educability, and decide that men and women
are still only half-rational descendants of the higher apes,
driven by animal instincts and passions, who are safe to
themselves and their fellows only if they are kept in chains.

We are concerned here with Christian doctrine and not
with political theory, and I must resist the temptation to follow this line of thought any further. What I want to make
plain at this stage is that the failure of political rationalism,
so far from constituting a *prima facie* disproof of Christian
dogma, is precisely what one would expect if man is what
Christian dogma asserts him to be. For, to put the matter
quite simply, the Christian view of evil in man is that, in
both the scholastic and the popular sense of the term, it is an
accident. That is to say, it is not something proper to man as
man, but is the result of a misfortune that has happened to
him.

Before going any further it will be well to get out of the

way the problem that is sometimes alleged to be raised by
what is misleadingly called "metaphysical evil," that is to say,
by the limitations upon a finite being's activity that arise directly from its finitude and particularity. For Christian theology this is no problem at all, though there is a good deal
of significance in the fact that people have supposed it to be
one. There is a story of a philosopher who, when asked why
an omnipotent providence permitted a dog to be tormented
by fleas, replied that they were given to it in order to prevent it from worrying about the fact that it was only a dog.
Whether or not the philosopher was clear-headed, the dog
as he conceived it was certainly not. For there is nothing to
trouble any creature in the fact that it is the sort of creature that it is; we have, I hope, seen this already. Only God
is infinite, every creature is of necessity finite; and if it is
finite it is finite in some particular kind of way. It is a perfectly good thing for a dog to be a dog, for a man to be a
man, for an angel to be an angel. It is, in fact, a perfectly
good thing for a creature to be a creature. If, however, a
creature is stupid enough not to be satisfied with being the
sort of creature that it is, and in particular if it is not satisfied with being a creature, everything is far from well. And
in fact it is just this last kind of dissatisfaction which the
Christian tradition sees as being the ultimate cause of evil
in the genuine and serious sense of the word.

For Christianity affirms that evil arises from sin in the
angelic world, in that realm of incorporeal beings whose
dazzling spirituality and transparent intellectuality, while
leaving them uncompromisingly within the created order,
nevertheless places them at its summit. The life of such
a being should consist in a changeless activity of pure praise,

in which its consciousness of its own radiant splendour will lead it only to glorify the God from whose creative love its own existence proceeds and whose infinite perfection its own finite perfection reflects. For such a being, it would appear, only two kinds of self-vitiation are fundamentally possible. Contemplating its own splendour, it may rebel against receiving this splendour from another, or it may pretend to itself that it does not receive it from another at all. That is to say, it may either rebel against being subject to God or deny that it is subject to him. Indeed, these two perversions are closely related, for corruption of the will invariably issues in clouding of the intellect and the two are in fact merely the voluntary and the intellectual aspect of the same distortion of the spirit. Thus, the radical sin of the fallen angels is pride, and any other sins, such as disobedience, of which they are guilty, follow upon it and are included in it.

I have briefly outlined the classical Christian doctrine of the fall of the angels for three reasons. First, because in the angels, whose pure spirituality is uncomplicated by the ramifications and elaborations that his dual psycho-physical constitution introduces in the case of man, the fundamental character of sin can be seen in its stark and horrible nakedness. It is the denial by a creature of the basic truth about itself, namely its dependence upon God, and the carrying of that denial into action. It is the deliberate adoption by a creature of the basic lie of all lies, and the incorporation of that lie into the creature's intellect and will. But, however much it may attempt to do so, the creature cannot in fact destroy its creaturehood, for that is held in God's hand and not in its own. If God did in fact endorse the creature's denial of its creaturehood, the creature would cease to exist;

for there are only two ways in which created existence could
cease to be created existence, either by losing its createdness,
which is impossible, or by losing its existence, which is annihilation. God, in his mercy, refuses to endorse the creature's
denial. Sin is thus, in its essence, an attempt to undo the
creative act of God, but just because that act is wholly
God's, the creature cannot undo it. All it can do is to delude
itself into the belief that it possesses a self-existence and a
self-sufficiency which in fact it does not possess. Its denial
of the truth can corrode both the intellect and the will but
cannot penetrate to the ontological root, where it draws
its very existence from the creative activity of God. It may
behave as if it were its own God, it may even persuade itself
that this is what it is, but it can never *be* this. Thus, as C. S.
Lewis has shown through the admirable literary medium of
his *Screwtape Letters*, the enterprise of the fallen angels is
fundamentally irrational; it does not make sense. One consequence is that the devils, though they may make use of
specious arguments when it suits their purpose, in order to
seduce human beings, have no respect for reason itself; and
indeed they can only render their existence tolerable at all
by their refusal ever to look the facts in the face. All that
hell is really concerned with is results, and short-term results
at that, since it has chosen the losing side. As that great Christian poet and thinker Charles Williams was fond of saying,
"Hell is inaccurate." [5]

My second reason for referring to the fall of the angels is
that it provides as good an explanation as we could have of
the fact that, if the indications of modern biological science
can be relied upon, the world seems to have got badly out
of joint before man arrived in it. We saw in the first chapter

that there is a definite path which can be traced through the ramifications of the evolutionary maze and which leads to man. Nevertheless, if we look at the process as a whole, we certainly receive the impression that there is a great deal of deformation, frustration, and suffering, both in the main path and in the "blind alleys," which requires explanation. It is just conceivable that this impression is erroneous, and we ought in any case, as C. E. Raven has reminded us,[6] to beware of assuming that wild animals experience pain or frustration in anything like the way in which we do; their cerebral structure does not seem to make that possible. However, in so far as the evolutionary process may have been distorted before the advent of man, it is reasonable to explain this distortion by the common Christian doctrine that one of the functions which God has committed to the angels is the supervision of the lower creation, so that the defection of certain of the angels has had as one of its consequences a disorganisation of the material world and the dislocation of its functions. This, too, has been given admirable imaginative expression by Lewis in his novels *Out of the Silent Planet* and *Perelandra*. The belief which was widespread in the Greco-Roman world of the first century and which is adopted without question by the New Testament, that the material world has fallen under the control of cosmic influences which are partly obtuse and partly malevolent—the "weak and beggarly rudiments of the world," [7] "the world-rulers of this darkness," [8] "the prince of the power of the air" [9] and so on—this belief would seem to be simply the expression, in the linguistic idiom of the period, of a profound intuition in the human soul that the very powers that direct the working of the material universe are perverted. If in comparison little is said about the unfallen spirits, this is readily explained by the fact that *their* activity, being wholly in line with and subject to the activity of God himself, need not in general be distinguished from the latter. For the same reason, and not because of a morbid preoccupation with the evil and the diabolic, much more is said about evil spirits than about good ones in works of ascetic and mystical theology.

My third reason is that both the Jewish and the Christian religions have been led to interpret the story of man's fall in the third chapter of Genesis as describing how man was seduced by a fallen angel from his obedience to God. Nothing would seem more likely than that a fallen angel would make such an attempt, and would make it at the first opportunity. For, as Lewis' devil Screwtape says, contrasting the plan of the devils with that of their enemy, God:

To us a human is primarily food; our aim is the absorption of its will into ours, the increase of our own area of selfhood at its expense. But the obedience which the Enemy demands of men is quite a different thing. One must face the fact that all the talk about his love for men, and his service being perfect freedom, is not (as one would gladly believe) mere propaganda, but an appalling truth. He really *does* want to fill the universe with a lot of loathsome little replicas of himself—creatures whose life, on its miniature scale, will be qualitatively like his own, not because he has absorbed them but because their wills freely conform to his. We want cattle who can finally become food; he wants servants who can finally become sons. We want to suck in, he wants to give out. We are empty and would be filled; he is full and flows over. Our war aim is a world in which Our Father Below has drawn all other beings into himself; the Enemy wants a world full of beings united to him but still distinct.[10]

I do not think I have anywhere found such a clear, and at the same time frightening, description as this, of the essentially predatory and insatiable character of the evil will, the will which desires everything except the one thing that can really satisfy it, because it desires everything for itself.

Space will not suffice me here to give a detailed account and defence of the traditional theology of the nature and consequences of the fall of man.[11] There are, however, several important points which must be briefly emphasised.

First, it seems to me to be both unnecessary and confusing to set in opposition the mythological and historical interpretations of the narrative of the fall in Genesis; that is to say, to take the narrative as an allegorical description of the nature of human sin as such, while denying that it can be taken as even an allegorical description of the first human sin. After all, if the narrative describes the nature of sin as such, it must describe the nature of the first sin; what is true of every member of a collection is true of any particular member. This could hardly be denied, but what is, I think, often denied—at any rate by implication—is that any special signification attaches to the first human sin just because it is the first. This denial is, I am convinced, quite mistaken. Whether the sin of Adam, to give the first human sin its traditional name, involved more malice in the will than subsequent sins is not, so far as I can see, either easy or important to know; and that is in any case a matter between Adam and his Creator. It does, however, seem to me to be obvious that the first human sin has an absolutely pivotal and catastrophic character, simply because it is the first. For, unless there was a previous fall on the part of rational corporeal beings in some part of the universe to us unknown, it constitutes the first occasion on which the material part of the universe has contravened God's will for it, and thus violated the law of its own being, by action originating from within itself. And in any case it constitutes the first such occasion emanating from within the realm of man. Like a microscopic crack in a china vase, it initiated a process of disintegration and corruption whose consequences spread far beyond the area of their origin and affected the whole subsequent history of the human race and of the material realm.

Second, I suggest that we should see the primary effect of Adam's fall as consisting essentially in a breaking of unity: first of all the breaking of Adam's own unity with God, and then the weakening of the unity which would otherwise have bound him and his descendants together in an organic body and have bound that organic body in unity with God. Subsequent sins may still further weaken that unity, subsequent acts of virtue may do something to repair it, but the fundamental and radical breach remains. The human race at the beginning of its history lost its true unity with God. In consequence, it has lost the unity which it was meant to have in itself, so that men are in conflict with one another. And as a further consequence its members have lost their own internal unity, so that in each man his passions and instincts, instead of working together harmoniously for his welfare and God's glory, pull him apart in their several directions and cause frustration and misery. When original sin—to use the technical term—is seen in this way, the problem of the mechanism of its transmission, which has so much worried theologians, evaporates. No special means of transmission is needed, other than human nature itself; just as no medium is needed for the transmission of the crack other than the material of the vase. This negative doctrine of original sin does not, of course, in the least belittle its gravity, for it extends in its effects to every element of man's nature and every department of his activity.

But as my third point I must note that the one thing which even sin cannot do to man, any more than it could do it to an angel, is utterly to destroy man's ontological contact with his Creator. Placed as he is in a world composed of God's creatures, his sins usually consist in choosing things that are in themselves good but which God does not wish him to have, or to have in a particular way, rather than in deliberately rebelling against God in sheer pride and malice. But even if he deliberately and with full advertence imitates the sin of Satan, even if on the moral level he tries, as it were, to undo his creation by repudiating and denying his dependence upon God, he cannot in fact undo it on the ontological level. "Those who deny thee," chants the chorus in T. S. Eliot's *Murder in the Cathedral*, "could not deny, if thou didst not exist; and their denial is never complete, for if it were so they would not exist." And it is this indestructible contact which even the fallen creature has with its Creator that provides the possibility of redemption. Without it the doctrine of redemption would be quite irrational.

For, and this is my fourth point, those versions of Christianity which deny that there is anything at all of value in fallen man implicitly deny the doctrine of creation. H. R. Mackintosh has written of Kierkgaard: "He can definitely be quoted for the view that our whole existence in time, the relativity in which we live as creatures who are not God, is *per se* guilty." [12] Similarly, Reinhold Niebuhr has written of the earlier teaching of Karl Barth: "The emphasis upon the difference between the holiness of God and the sinfulness of man is so absolute that man is convicted, not of any particular breaches against the life of the humanity community, but of being human and not divine. Thus, to all intents and purposes, creation and the fall are identified." [13] And Anders Nygren, following in the footsteps of Luther, sees the essence of the Protestant case against Catholicism as consisting simply in the affirmation that, even with the aid of grace, there is no way from man to God and that, even with the aid of grace, man can have no fellowship with God on the level of God's holiness, though he can have fellowship with God on the basis of sin.[14]

Three distinct questions are in fact involved here, though they are very rarely distinguished. There is first the question whether man has any value as created and unfallen, second the question whether man has any value as fallen and unredeemed, and third the question whether man has any value when he has been redeemed by God. Theoretically, it would be perfectly possible to hold that man as created was of value, but that he lost this value through his fall. And then it might be held either that this value was recovered by redemption or that it was not. Protestantism of the type just quoted would seem to deny value to man in all three situations, but they are not commonly distinguished with sufficient clarity for this to be altogether certain in most cases. There is, I think, a reason for this lack of discrimination, and it is that, for strict Protestantism, the essence of the fall consists in the creature attributing value to itself. The Catholic retort, that there is nothing wrong in a creature attributing value to itself so long as it recognises that this value is wholly derived from God, will seem to classical Protestant theology to be nothing but a sophistry. For, as Père Bouyer has recently shown, the nominalist outlook which both sides in the sixteenth century inherited from medievalism in decay makes it impossible to hold that anything whatever can really inhere in a creature and at the same time be wholly a gift from God.[15] (May I hasten to repeat that Protestant religion is often very different from Protestant theology?) In any case, whatever may be the view of man as unfallen, there can be no doubt that man as fallen has been viewed by traditional Protestantism as destroyed beyond repair. He may be accounted righteous in view of the merits of Christ, he may even perform moral and religious acts as a result of the favour with which God now regards him, but in himself he remains the valueless object which he was before, *simul justus et peccator*, essentially sinful, though now accounted righteous on account of Christ's merits which he has grasped by faith.

Against this whole attitude I wish to maintain two theses. The first, upon which I have already touched, is that there is no incompatibility between man's inherent value and his total dependence upon God. To be a creature is, as I have argued elsewhere, neither to be unreal on the one hand nor to be self-existent on the other, but to exist with a *dependent reality*.[16] Hence the fundamental sin does not consist in recognising and rejoicing in one's own value, but in refusing to recognise the source from which it comes and to glorify its Giver for his gift. And second, even when sin has occurred, although the will, having turned its back upon God, is powerless to reorient itself towards him, the basic ontological act by which God maintains the creature in existence still persists and provides the foundation for the further act by which God can reorient it towards himself. To use the scholastic terms, man is *spoliatus gratuitis et vulneratus in naturalibus*. He has lost the loving intercourse with the Father which he once enjoyed and all the graces and blessings which flowed from it, and in consequence of this loss even his natural capacities have been wounded and weakened. Nevertheless, his fundamental natural endowments remain. He can make intellectual progress, though it is a laborious and painful process, marked by many obstacles and divagations; the astounding scientific movement of the last four centuries is the most striking example of this. He can even make moral progress, though this is a much more ambiguous business and much more difficult to assess. But all this progress is dogged and infected by a radical frustration and decay. The fruit that appeared so beautiful, was longed for so earnestly, and was striven for so painfully, turns to ashes in the mouth. Even when what looked to be good turns out to be good in fact, there is evil mingled with it. G. K. Chesterton wrote to his fiancée:

I like the Cyclostyle ink; it is so inky. I do not think there is anyone who takes quite such a fierce pleasure in things being themselves as I do. The startling wetness of water excites and intoxicates me: the fieriness of fire, the steeliness of steel, the unutterable muddiness of mud. It is just the same with people.[17]

And yet it was this same Chesterton who declared, in words which I have already quoted, that "there is a spirit abroad among the nations of the earth which drives men incessantly on to destroy what they cannot understand, and to capture what they cannot enjoy."

That man is still good, and yet not wholly good; that he is capable of acts of astounding generosity and self-sacrifice, and also of acts of almost diabolical cruelty and perversion; that his best acts have an evil twist in them, and that his worst acts reveal a glimmer of good—all this is simply a matter of experience. And neither the cynic nor the sentimentalist is facing the facts as they actually are. The optimist, it has been said, proclaims that we live in the best of all possible worlds, and the pessimist is afraid that this is true. Or again, the optimist thinks everything is good except the pessimist, while the pessimist thinks everything is bad except himself. It has also been remarked that a pessimist is a man who has to live with an optimist. And over against both these rather ridiculous figures, against the pessimist with his cynicism and the optimist with his sentimentalism, we have to set the figure of the Christian realist, the man who recognises things as they are, who discerns and acclaims the fundamental goodness of the world and at the same time frankly recognises its accidental badness; who acknowledges man's helplessness and also God's power to help him.

The doctrine of original sin, it has often been remarked, is a thoroughly cheerful doctrine, for it enables us to look the facts in the face without losing hope. The two chief sins against hope, the text-books tell us, are presumption and despair, and they are the two characteristic sins of the optimist and the pessimist respectively. Into which of them we are more likely to fall will depend very much upon the circumstances: upon our temperament and our fortunes, the social environment and the political era in which we live. At the present day, we are perhaps more likely to fall into pessimism than into optimism, after the shock of two world wars and the even more menacing threats to civilisation that have developed in the postwar period. The doctrine of original sin *is* a cheerful doctrine, for it assures us that the sad condition in which we find ourselves is not the condition for which we are made and that by the grace of God we can be delivered from it. It is, however, important to remember that, while original sin manifests itself upon the empirical level in human frustration of all kinds—political, social, and psychological—it is in its essence religious, it consists in a vitiated relation to God. It can therefore be as deadly and corroding in societies and epochs which are prosperous and stable as in those that are impoverished and precarious, in men and women who are psychologically healthy as in those who are neurotic or deranged. We have seen a good deal in recent years of an evangelistic technique which begins by trying to frighten men with the hydrogen bomb and then offers Christianity as a means of deliverance. As V. A. Demant has pointed out, such an approach is religiously illicit and politically dangerous; religiously illicit because "if sin is a universal human condition, it is there in peaceful food-gathering tribes and in relatively tranquil periods like the nineteenth century," and politically dangerous because it suggests that it is not worth while to work for social justice and political order until the world has been converted. In Demant's words:

The difference between a decent political order and chaos of destruction is not the difference between a converted and a sinful world. It is the difference between a civilised and an uncivilised sinful one. And if the only prophylactic against world-destruction is universal conversion, no one is going to bother to work for a little more justice in a naughty world.[18]

It is precisely because man's nature is wounded by sin that Christian social action is necessary; but it is because man's nature is not destroyed by sin that Christian social action is possible. This does not affect the specifically religious issue. It is because man has fallen from grace that conversion is necessary; but it is because grace both heals and transforms nature that his restoration is possible. However, this will bring us to the subject of our concluding chapter.

VI · MAN IN CHRIST

In the preceding chapters I have attempted to show that finite beings, as totally dependent for their existence and their nature upon the incessant creative activity of God, are by this very fact capable of becoming the objects of a further, supervenient divine activity, which will evoke from them potentialities that they cannot actualise for themselves, will raise them to an order of being above the natural level, and will cure such wounds as nature may have incurred through sin. Furthermore, if they are rational beings bearing upon themselves the image of their Creator, their elevation will consist in a participation in the very life of God himself which, if it proceeds to its proper end, will culminate in the beatific vision in heaven. To use the technical theological terms, nature can be perfected, elevated, and healed by grace. Nature can be supernaturalised; fallen nature can be restored. This supernatural activity of God, which nature has no inherent right either to demand or to expect, but which nature can appropriate if God extends it, might very well operate—if it operates at all—by a direct action of God upon the creature without any kind of intermediary. Indeed, this may be what happens in those cases,

of whose existence it seems impossible to doubt, wherein
the obvious fruits of supernatural union with God are produced in the lives of men and women who are not even pro-
fessing Christians and may never have heard of the Christian religion. A conspicuous example is that of the great
Islamic Sufi mystic Al-Hallaj, whose case has been discussed
in detail by Louis Massignon and Père Joseph Maréchal,[1]
and it could be paralleled, perhaps less spectacularly, by
many others. *Facienti quod in se est Deus non denegat gra-
tiam* is a theological commonplace. However, this purely
individual union with God, which in his mercy he sees fit
to grant to those who can profit by it, is something far less
rich and ample than the corporate and organic supernaturalisation which is offered to us as members of Christ in the
mystical body of the sacramental Church. It is this that I
shall try to expound in this concluding chapter.

There was in the Middle Ages a lively controversy between theologians on the question whether the Second Person of the Holy Trinity would have become incarnate if
man had not sinned and so had not needed redemption. The
Scotist school maintained that the Incarnation would have
taken place in any case, in order that manhood might be
raised to a new dignity and receive enhanced privileges
through its assumption by the divine Word; so august a
mystery as the Incarnation, it was felt, ought not to be con-
tingent upon so squalid, and in the last resort unnecessary,
an event as the Fall. The Thomist school, on the other hand,
inclined to the opinion that the Incarnation was directly
concerned with redemption, and held that Scripture war-
ranted no wider view. The controversy is largely an academic

one, for man has in fact fallen, and the Thomists were as anxious as the Scotists to insist that in actual fact the Incarnation has not only redeemed man but has also provided the means of his supernaturalisation; and in any case we must presume that God, in his supra-temporal omniscience, foresaw and provided for events as they have actually happened. However difficult may be the intellectual problems that are involved, Christian theology maintains that there is no ultimate contradiction between the omniscience of God and the freedom of man. My present concern is thus to point out that, while God might (and in many cases no doubt does) confer grace by a simple extension and augmentation of the act by which he confers existence, the covenanted and public vehicle of grace is the human nature taken by God the Son; and, furthermore, that this dispensation on the part of God is coherent and congruous with the essentially social nature of man.

The Incarnation is in itself a great wonder and a great mystery. "Of all the works of God," writes St. Thomas, "it most greatly surpasses our reason; for nothing more wonderful could be thought of that God could do than that very God, the Son of God, should become very man." [2] If one is content to view the human nature of Christ as a mere phantom appearance, after the manner of the Docetic heretics of the early centuries, there is nothing very much in the Incarnation to draw forth either our wonder or our awe; nor is there if, with some of the oriental religions, we look upon God and nature as essentially identical. But if, with orthodox Christianity, we hold both that Godhead and manhood are radically distinct and also that Christ is truly both God and man, the Incarnation becomes, if not a self-contradiction, at any rate a mystery of the most surpassing wonder.

> Behold, the world's Creator wears
> The form and fashion of a slave;
> Our very flesh our Maker shares,
> His fallen creature, man, to save.
>
> .   .   .   .
>
> He shrank not from the oxen's stall,
> He lay within the manger-bed,
> And he whose bounty feedeth all
> At Mary's breast himself was fed.[3]

This doctrine of the *Verbum supernum prodiens nec linquens Patris dexteram* [4]—of the Word of God, who proceeds forth and yet leaves not the Father's side—is not in fact nonsensical, for the infinite can contain the finite, without the infinite being changed or the finite destroyed; but it is a most wonderful and profound mystery. And theologians have seen the union of manhood with the Person of the Son of God in the Incarnation as providing the supreme example of the supernaturalisation of nature by grace, for there is no way conceivable by which human nature could be so ineffably exalted as by becoming the very medium in which God himself lives the life of man.

Thus, in the Incarnation we see the supreme honour conferred by God upon human nature; in no way could God have honoured it more than by himself becoming man. Yet we must not allow ourselves to think of the Incarnation in purely honorific terms. God became man not simply in order to honour mankind, but to perfect and elevate and heal it. He was not like a monarch condescending to accept the diploma of a degree from a university within his own kingdom; he became man, as the Nicene Creed briefly but pungently says, "for us men and for our salvation." The Incarnation is thus a fact of crucial significance for the human race. "He became man," writes St. Athanasius quite simply, "in order that we might become God." [5] And in saying this the great African doctor does not of course mean that we lose our creaturely status, but that, remaining creatures, we are, as a consequence of the Incarnation, made sharers in the life of God.

Theologians in Western Christendom have laid great stress upon the expiatory aspect of the Incarnation, that is to say upon the fact that, by his life of perfect love and obedience, with its culmination in his death upon the Cross, Christ made a perfect reparation for the offence that human sin had inflicted upon the holiness and the majesty of God. He "made there," says the consecration prayer of the Anglican liturgy, "a full, perfect and sufficient sacrifice, oblation and satisfaction for the sins of the whole world." And this indeed must never be forgotten. By far the worst aspect of sin, objectively considered, is the insult that it offers to man's Creator. However, if this aspect is treated as all-inclusive, we are in danger of overlooking or belittling the fact that in the Incarnation God was not concerned in the first place to vindicate his own dignity but to rescue man from the consequences of man's malice and obstinacy: "the Son of man came to seek and to save that which was lost." [6] Furthermore, we shall find it difficult to escape from the crudest substitutionary view of the Atonement. "Man has sinned, man must pay the penalty, so God the Son became man and paid it. However, the man who paid it was not one of the men who sinned; therefore we can only suppose that God, by a kind of legal fiction, attributes Christ's merits to us." Clearly we must find some more genuine link than this between Christ and ourselves if redemption is—I will not say "to be explained" (for to explain this great mystery may well be beyond our grasp) but—not to seem frankly nonsensical and immoral.

When we turn to the New Testament, although it is true that we find a very deliberate emphasis laid upon the fact that Christ has made reparation for our sins, we see this fact placed in a far wider context, that of the re-creation and re-assembling of the ruined and scattered human race. Christ "cancelled the bond which stood against us with its legal demands; this he set aside, nailing it to the Cross." [7] This is very true. But he also died that he might "gather into one the children of God who are scattered abroad." [8] And he is the Second Adam, the ancestor of the new human race whose other name is the Body of Christ.

Lionel Thornton, in his profound and elaborate treatise *Revelation and the Modern World*, has shown the way in which this great Pauline theme was taken up and developed in the thought of St. Irenaeus of Lyons, the first great theologian of the Christian Church after the time of the apostles. For Irenaeus, "creation and redemption are parts of a single plan." "He who feeds our bodies with his flesh and blood in the Eucharist is also he who makes provision for the earthly needs of those same bodies in the order of creation." [9] "Creation, Scripture and the Church are so fused into one whole that, although we can and must distinguish them, yet they cannot be separated." [10] With a wealth of illustration, Thornton shows how this Pauline and Irenaean doctrine of Christ as the Second Adam, solidly based as it is on Scripture, implies that in Christ creation is both restored and fulfilled. To Hebrew thought and to biblical thought in general there is a real identity between a man and his descendants; they are, so to speak, "included" in him. Thus, when, by birth from a human mother, God the Son, who is Adam's Creator, becomes as man one of Adam's descendants, he recreates and restores the human race. "Adam is the 'whole' to which all men belong; and Christ is the whole to which all are transferred by inclusion of Adam in Christ." [11] Much more is, however, to be seen here than the mere adoption by St. Paul or St. Irenaeus of the anthropological or biological outlook of first-century Judaism, an outlook which we of the twentieth century might well be inclined to reject as outmoded and unscientific. To quote Thornton again:

It is now widely recognised that in the Pauline treatment of the comparison between Adam and Christ the details of the comparison are determined not so much by theories about Adam as by the significance of the revelation in Christ. In other words, Christian beliefs were not subordinated to contemporary ideas. On the contrary, current notions about Adam were adapted to fit the primitive apostolic Christology. As a magnet, by its mere presence, draws to itself objects in the environment which are amenable to its influence, so did the gospel of Christ, through the medium of those who acknowledged its sway, draw into its orbit materials of its cultural and intellectual environment lying ready to hand. Again, as the magnet supports the objects which are attached to it, so too did the gospel of Christ hold together the materials thus drawn into its orbit, thereby giving to those materials a new unity of form through which its own significance could be expressed.[12]

We have already seen that the primary effect of the first human sin—an effect which every subsequent sin has extended and intensified—was to break at its beginning the threefold unity which the human race was meant to enjoy: the unity of man with God, the unity of man with man, and the unity of man within himself. This unity is reestablished and reintroduced when the Creator, becoming man by birth from a human mother, refashions upon his own figure the substance of fallen man. In his own individuality this refashioning is complete; he is the perfect Man, the totally obedient Son of the Father, and in his individual manhood he makes to the Father that perfect offering which Adam had failed to make. In him manhood has become altogether *filial,* and filial as Adam's never was. For even if Adam had not sinned, his filiality would have been a purely created filiality; whereas in Christ human nature has been raised to a share in that eternal and divine filiality which the Son exercises in the life of the Holy Trinity. In Jesus of Nazareth, then, manhood is restored to sonship by being raised to a sonship that it never had before; nature is perfected by being supernaturalised. This is itself an event of supreme significance for the whole human race, which is, as it were, bathed in and infused with the radiance that streams from the human nature of the Incarnate Lord.

There the matter might have remained, had God not decided to do some even greater thing for us, namely to give us the means of being incorporated into the human nature which the Son assumed, so that we should not be merely bathed in a radiance poured upon us from without but be taken up into its very source. By incorporation into Christ we become sons of God by adoption. The sonship which was imparted to his own individual human nature by the Incarnation is imparted to us by our incorporation into him. Thus the grace which the Christian receives, while it elevates him into the life of God and, in the scriptural phrase, makes him "a partaker of the divine nature," [13] does this by the specific means of communicating to him, by his incorporation into Christ, the sonship which the Son of God enjoys in the Holy Trinity. We become sons in the Son. "Because you are sons," writes St. Paul, "God has sent the Spirit of his Son into our hearts crying, 'Abba, Father!' So through God you are no longer a slave but a son, and if a Son then an heir." [14] "God, who is rich in mercy . . . made us alive together with Christ (by grace you have been saved), and raised us up with him, and made us sit with him in the heavenly places in Christ Jesus." [15] This is nothing less than a new act of creation. "We are his workmanship, created in Christ Jesus." [16] "If any one is in Christ, he is a new creation." [17] This new creation does not imply that the old creation is destroyed, but that it is renewed and perfected: "The old things are passed away; behold, they are become new." [18]

Since the Christian, through his union with Christ, is lifted up into the life of the Trinity, he himself enjoys the gift of the Spirit which the Father eternally bestows upon the Son: "Because you are sons, God has sent the Spirit of his Son into our hearts." [19] And those who are incorporated into Jesus are inevitably united with one another: "We, though many, are one body in Christ, and individually members one of another." [20] To use the phrase of the Anglican Book of Common Prayer, we are made very members incorporate of Christ's mystical body; thus Christ in his totality consists not just of Jesus of Nazareth but of Jesus and his Church, the

Head and his members: "just as the body is one and has many
members, and all the members of the body, though many,
are one body, so also is Christ [not "are Christians"]. For
by one Spirit we were all baptised into one body—Jews or
Greeks, slaves or free—and all were made to drink of one
Spirit." [21] Thus, in the Christian Church—the Body of
Christ—mankind has recovered the unity that it lost in Adam
and has indeed been granted a more wonderful and interior
unity than it had lost. This is unity far deeper than any
visible unity of human association, and it is a unity which
can persist even when, as has happened through the sins
of Christians, the visible unity of human association has
been destroyed; for it is nothing less than a participation in
the unity which binds together the Persons of the Holy
Trinity, the unity for which the Lord Jesus prayed on the
night before his passion: "That they may all be one, even as
thou, Father, art in me, and I in thee, that they also may be
in us." [22]

We are now in a position to see, more clearly than was
possible before, the nature of the progress which man is
called upon to undertake now that, to use Julian Huxley's
words, "the evolutionary process, as now embodied in
man, has for the first time become aware of itself, is studying
the laws of its own unfolding, and has a dawning realisation
of the possibilities of its future guidance or control." [23] We
have already seen that the Christian, remembering that God
has himself become man, can only say that he wants man to
remain man. But now, remembering that the Christian has
been incorporated by his baptism into the manhood which
God has taken, we can go on to say that the only kind
of consciously directed human evolution which we can

recognise as fully valid is evolution within the Body of Christ; that is to say, the progressive incorporation of the human race into the sacramental Church, and the development and use of all man's newly won powers under the governing influence of supernatural grace as the body grows "to mature manhood, to the measure of the stature of the fulness of Christ." [24] In this way, and only in this way, can the gigantic scientific and technological achievements of which, in our modern world, fallen human nature has shown itself to be so amazingly and alarmingly capable, be made ancillary to man's supernatural life and destiny, and also be reoriented and transformed by the vitalising operation of grace. It is only in so far as man's natural powers are taken up into the supernatural order that the venom which has infected them can be drawn from them and that they can become fully instrumental to the true welfare of the human race.

But, it will be objected, all this is sheer romanticism. What conceivable likelihood is there that, in any foreseeable future, our modern industrial civilisation will abdicate from the titanic status of self-sufficiency which it has appropriated and, like the Magi of old, lay its gifts in humble adoration at the feet of the Incarnate Word? Can we for one moment imagine our Western democracies, to say nothing of Soviet Russia and the increasingly industrialised nations of Asia and Africa, deliberately and joyfully directing their political, social, and technological organisations to the building up of the Body of Christ? If this is all that Christianity has to offer in the face of the menace of nuclear war, it might as well withdraw from all concern with the social field. Did we not see in the last chapter that the proclamation of universal

conversion as the necessary and sufficient instrument for the
solving of the world's immediate political and social problems is both unsound from the standpoint of theology and
unrealistic and dangerous from the point of view of practical politics?

I do not think, however, that this objection is valid. Whatever may be the case in a professedly Christian social order,
in a secularised order such as that in which we live today
the Church's influence has to be exercised in two ways: first,
by safeguarding and encouraging in every possible way
those natural tendencies and powers which, in spite of their
weakening and distortion by sin, are not entirely destroyed
by sin and the Fall; and second, by simply living the supernatural life of the Body of Christ in the midst of the secularised world. In spite of the time that has elapsed since it was
written in 1934, there is, I believe, much for us to learn from
the discussion in Jacques Maritain's *True Humanism* of
the peculiar role of the Church in a secular (the French
word is *profane*) society. And, vital as it is for Christians to
take an active and informed part in the life of the community and not to retreat from the hard realities of the
twentieth century into a warm and cosy enclave of re-
ligiosity, the fact remains that the supreme social service
which the Church can perform—and one which can be per-
formed by no other agency—is the living of the Church's
life as the redeemed sacramental community in the midst
of a civilisation whose activities, whether beneficent or harm-
ful, are for the most part organised for entirely secular ends.
For the grace which is mediated through the sacramental
activity of the Body of Christ is not limited in its objects

and its effects by the Church's visible boundaries. To quote
some words which I have written elsewhere:

Because Christ died for the whole world and commissioned
his Church to preach the Gospel to all the nations, the Church's
sacramental life is the means by which not only the affairs of
Christians but of all men are brought under the mercy and the
grace of God. The sacrifice which the Mass perpetuates was
offered for the sins of the whole world as their full, perfect and
sufficient sacrifice, oblation and satisfaction. The grace which
God pours into the Church through the sacraments overflows
the Church's visible boundaries and floods the whole of creation
with its regenerative power. It brings under the eyes of God all
human misery and suffering, it claims for God every act of human love, it pleads God's mercy for every act of human selfish-
ness and hate, it claims all God's creation as his possession.[25]

Thus, however prone Christians are at times to forget it,
the sacramental life of the Church both floods with divine
grace the world at large and also, by the very universality of
its operation, declares that the place where men are meant to
be is not outside the Church but within. Thus, even if it is
possible for men to receive grace and to achieve salvation
outside the Church as it is visibly manifested on earth, this
does not mean that membership in the Church is unimportant.
For the basic question with which a man is concerned is not
"What must I do to be saved?" but "Lord, what wouldst
thou have me to do?" There are, of course, complicated
questions about the nature and the limits of the Church on
which Christians are notoriously and lamentably at vari-
ance; they lie outside the scope of this book. But one
thing at least is clear from the New Testament, that no one
can be a Christian in isolation. Even if his membership of the

Church is invisible, the Church itself is a visible reality; and, if not here, then in the Resurrection at the last day, a man must be a member of Christ's body if he is to be a member of Christ, and he must be a member of Christ if he is to be a son of God.

In making these exalted claims for the Church, there is, of course, no suggestion that its members are themselves free from defects. When a man is incorporated into Christ, this is the beginning of his sanctification, not its end. Nevertheless, in its inner reality, as distinct from its empirical manifestation, the Church is the spotless and redeemed bride of Christ, the New Jerusalem come down from heaven to earth, without spot or wrinkle or any such thing.[26] To continue my above quotation:

To outward view the Church may appear to be merely a rather queer gathering of very miscellaneous men and women, inexplicably preoccupied with old-fashioned ceremonies, strangely excited about apparently irrelevant issues, and patently failing to live in accordance with the ideals of human life in which they profess to believe. But in its inner reality the Church is the re-created human race, the holy people of God, the divine community in which the Son of God patiently and tenderly draws men and women into his own perfect human nature and offers them to the Father as his members made one with him and clothed with his glory. Such is the Church of God, black with the sins of its members but comely with the beauty and holiness of its Head, and of this Church the sacraments are the very life.

For it is through the sacraments that the Church militant here on earth, that lower fringe of the mystical Body of Christ to which we now belong, is constantly renewed by her glorified Head who has taken his human nature with him into the heavenly realm. If the Incarnation was only an episode in the life of the divine Word, if he became man at his conception but ceased to be man at his ascension, the doctrine of the Church and of the sacraments would be cut at its roots. It is because he is still man, though glorified by his resurrection and ascension in a way that we can hardly conceive, that men and women can be incorporated into his human nature today, and that the Church is truly, and not by a vague and inexact metaphor, the Body of Christ. And the bond of union between the glorified Body of the Redeemer in the heavenly realm and that part of his Mystical Body which is militant here on earth is the Sacramental Body of the Eucharist. For the essential reality by which the glorified, the Mystical and the Sacramental Body are constituted is one and the same; it is the human nature which, at his Incarnation, the Word of God took to himself, by the operation of the Holy Ghost, in the womb of his virgin mother Blessed Mary. Thus the Eucharist is the means by which the earthly Church is nourished and maintained, for in the Eucharist the Church's inner reality is communicated to her. It is, however, more than this. The Eucharist is also the prefiguration and the foretaste of the final glorification of the created universe, that glorification in which, through its complete incorporation into the manhood of Christ, manhood will receive the fulfilment of God's promise that all things will be put in subjection under its feet. In the final judgement of the last day, there can be only two alternatives for every man and woman, either to be totally in or to be totally outside the Body of Christ. In the mean time the ultimate destiny of many is as yet unsettled; incorporated into Christ by our baptism, we are still able either to co-operate with the grace of God or to resist it. In Christ by grace, we are still part of the fallen world by nature.

> *Sunt modo praelia, postmodo praemia. Qualia? Plena:*
> *Plena refectio, nullaque passio, nullaque poena.*
> *Spe modo vivitur, et Syon angitur a Babylone;*
> *Nunc tribulatio; tunc recreatio, sceptra, coronae.*
> *Qui modo creditur, ipse videbitur, atque scietur:*
> *Ipse videntibus atque scientibus attribuetur.*

> And now we fight the battle,
>   But then shall wear the crown
> Of full and everlasting
>   And passionless renown:
> And now we watch and struggle,
>   And now we live in hope,
> And Sion in her anguish
>   With Babylon must cope:
> But he whom now we trust in
>   Shall then be seen and known,
> And they that know and see him
>   Shall have him for their own.[27]

Nevertheless, by grace we have a real foretaste, a real participation, in the mode proper to our present pilgrim condition, of the glory that God has prepared for us. And by supernatural charity—the third and greatest of the theological virtues—we are each of us able to lay hold for ourselves of the virtues of our fellow Christians.

> *Licet cuiquam sit diversum pro labore meritum,*
> *Caritas hoc facit suum quod amat in altero;*
> *Proprium sic singulorum fit commune omnium.*

"Although each has a different merit according to his work,

yet charity makes her own that in which she rejoices in another; and so what is proper to each becomes common to all." In these words St. Peter Damian was describing the state of the blessed in heaven, but in their measure they are no less true of our union with each other in the mystical Body of Christ while we are militant here on earth. The way in which we can best appropriate to ourselves the holiness of the saints is not by envying them for their superior graces or even by deliberately trying to imitate them, but by rejoicing that they have glorified God in their lives so much better than we have in ours. By so rejoicing we shall be drawn closer to them and thus become more like them. And nowhere are we drawn closer to them and to each other than in the sacrament of the Eucharist which makes and preserves the unity of the Body of Christ.

Over against the dissatisfied "Acquisitive Man" and his no less avid successor the dehumanised "Mass-Man" of our economically focussed societies insecurely organised for time, Christianity sets the type of "Eucharistic Man"—man giving thanks with the product of his labours upon the gift of God, and daily rejoicing with his fellows in the worshipping society which is grounded in eternity. This is man to whom it was promised on the night before Calvary that he should henceforth eat and drink at the table of God and be a king.

Thus wrote Dom Gregory Dix in the preface to his great work *The Shape of the Liturgy*, and it is on this note that I should wish to leave my subject. We have considered only some aspects—but some of the most important aspects nevertheless—of the Christian doctrine of man. Man in his twofold nature of body and soul; man in his twofold orientation as an individual and a member of society; man with his nature perfected and transformed by its elevation to the order of supernature; man fallen and broken by sin but restored, and more than restored, in Christ who is both God and Man; man destined for the vision of God in eternity, and destined for it as a member of the total Christ; man here and now given a foretaste of the final consummation by his participation in the Eucharistic sacrifice of the Lord's Body and Blood—this is the theme that I have tried to put before you in these lectures, but it is a theme to which only the tongues of angels could do justice. "There is one Son who fulfilled the Father's will," wrote St. Irenaeus, "and there is one human race in which the mysteries of God are fulfilled." [28] "What is man, that thou art mindful of him, or the son of man, that thou carest for him? Thou madest him for a little while lower than the angels; thou hast crowned him with glory and honour, putting everything in subjection under his feet."

NOTES

I. THE UNIQUENESS OF MAN

1. Hebrews ii.6–8, citing Psalm viii.4–6.
2. *Christian Theology and Natural Science*, pp. 36 f.
3. *Nature of the Physical World*, p. 178.
4. See Hoyle, *Frontiers of Astronomy*, p. 274.
5. Cf. Whitrow, *The Structure of the Universe*, p. 24.
6. *Frontiers of Astronomy*, p. 83.
7. *Christian Theology and Natural Science*, pp. 36 f.
8. "The Uniqueness of Man" is the first chapter in the book of the same title.
9. *Ibid.*, pp. 9 f.
10. *Ibid.*, p. 15 f.
11. *Le Phénomène humain*, p. 187.
12. "The Evolutionary Process," in Huxley and others, eds., *Evolution as a Process*, p. 13.
13. *Uniqueness of Man*, p. 32.
14. Genesis ii.7.
15. *Summa theologica*, I, xxii, 2 *ad* 1; cf. I, cxvi, 1c.
16. Isaiah lxv.11.
17. *Summa theologica*, I, ii, 3c.

II. BODY AND SOUL

1. "The Structure of the Brain and the Process of Thinking," in Laslett, ed., *The Physical Basis of Mind*, p. 23. The writer

clearly means to say that the weight of the human brain is two or three times the weight of the *brain* of the gorilla, not that it is two or three times the weight of the gorilla itself.

2. See Bertalanffy, *Problems of Life*, p. 86.
3. "The Evolutionary Process," in Huxley and others, eds., *Evolution as a Process*, pp. 12–13.
4. Pp. 51–53.   5. *Ibid.*, pp. 94–95.   6. P. 124.
7. *The Spirit of Medieval Philosophy*, p. 172.
8. See my *Christian Theology and Natural Science*, Chapter Three.

III. INDIVIDUAL AND SOCIETY

1. Much of the material in this chapter is reproduced, by permission of Faber and Faber, Ltd., from my essay "The Person and the Family," in Reckitt, ed., *Prospect for Christendom*.
2. *Contra Eutychen*, III, 4. Cf. St. Thomas Aquinas, *Summa theologica*, I, xxix, 1; and *De Potentia*, ix, 2.
3. *Summa theologica*, I, xxix, 3; cf. *De Potentia*, ix, 3.
4. *Scholasticism and Politics*, pp. 45 f.
5. *Ibid.*, p. 50.
6. *The Meaning of Love*, Part Two, section 5.
7. *Scholasticism and Politics*, p. 54.
8. *Ibid.*, p. 58.
9. *The Necessity of Belief*, p. 135.
10. *Religion and Culture*, p. 21.
11. Matthew xix.6. Cf. Genesis ii.24.
12. "The Preservation of Marriage," *Christendom* (December, 1937), p. 245.
13. "The Weight of Glory," *Theology* (November, 1941), p. 263.
14. Mersch, *Love, Marriage and Chastity;* Doms, *The Meaning of Marriage;* Hildebrand, *Die Ehe;* Wayne, *Morals and Marriage;* Bentley, "One Flesh," *Christendom* (March, 1940).
15. *Acta Apostolicae Sedis*, XXXVI, p. 103 (decree of March 30, 1944).

16. Encyclical *Casti connubii* of 1930; *A.A.S., XXII*, p. 548.
17. P. 168, and Chapter Fourteen.
18. *Ibid.*, p. 5.
19. See my *Christian Theology and Natural Science*, pp. 277 f.
20. *Ecclesiastical Polity*, V, lxxiii, 1.
21. *Sermon on the Marriage Ring.*
22. i.28.
23. Ephesians v.21 f.
24. P. 202.   25. *Ibid.*, p. 50.   26. *Ibid.*, p. 210.
27. *Beauty Looks after Herself* (facing title page).
28. *De Regimine Principum*, i. 14–15.

IV. NATURE AND SUPERNATURE

1. II Peter i.4.
2. See *The Christian Philosophy of St. Thomas Aquinas*, Part One, Chapter Four; and *Being and Some Philosophers*, passim.
3. *Via Media*, p. 153.
4. See my discussion of nominalism in *The Recovery of Unity*, pp. 19 f.
5. See *Summa theologica*, I, xii, 7 *ad* 3 (cf. *obj.* 3).
6. *Summa theologica*, I, xii, 7c.
7. John i.16.
8. *Summa theologica*, I, i, 8 *ad* 2.   9. *Ibid.*, I, ii, 2 *ad* 1.
10. *Deus deum te vult facere, non natura sed . . . adoptione. . . . Sic totus homo deificatus* (Serm. 166, 4).
11. "Filii in Filio," *Nouvelle Revue théologique* (July, 1938), p. 825.
12. *The Spirit and Forms of Protestantism*, pp. 155–56.
13. P. 88.
14. *Contra Nestorium et Eutychen*, II (Migne, P. G., LXXXVI, 1333).

V. MAN FALLEN

1. *The Social Contract*, II, v.
2. *Science and Common Sense*, p. 2.

3. *G. F. Watts*, p. 110.
4. *The Future of Industrial Man*, p. 137 (American ed., pp. 200–1).
5. Cited by Lewis in *Arthurian Torso*, p. 106.
6. *Natural Religion and Christian Theology*, II, 116.
7. Galatians iv.3, 9.   8. Ephesians vi.12.   9. Ephesians ii.2.
10. *The Screwtape Letters*, p. 45.
11. See my *Christ, the Christian and the Church*, pp. 154 f.; and *Christian Theology and Natural Science*, pp. 299 f.
12. *Types of Modern Theology*, p. 237.
13. *Moral Man and Immoral Society*, p. 68.
14. See *Agape and Eros*, p. 690, *passim*.
15. See *The Spirit and Forms of Protestantism*, Chapter Seven.
16. See my *Via Media*, Chapter One.
17. Cited by Ward, *Gilbert Keith Chesterton*, p. 97.
18. "Oxford Hears Billy Graham Again," *The Oxford Magazine* (November 24, 1955), p. 136.

VI. MAN IN CHRIST

1. See Maréchal, *Studies in the Psychology of the Mystics.*
2. *Summa contra Gentiles*, IV, xxvii.
3. *A solis ortus cardine*, trans. J. Ellerton.
4. St. Thomas Aquinas, Hymn for Corpus Christi.
5. *De Incarnatione*, 54.
6. Luke xix.10.   7. Colossians, ii.14.
8. John xi.52.
9. Thornton, *Revelation and the Modern World*, p. 120.
10. *Ibid.*, p. 125.
11. *Ibid.*, p. 152.
12. *Ibid.*, p. 148.
13. II Peter i.4.   14. Galatians iv.6, 7.   15. Ephesians ii.4–6.
16. Ephesians ii.10.   17. II Corinthians v.17.   18. *Ibid.*
19. Galatians iv.6.   20. Romans xii.4.
21. I Corinthians xii.13.   22. John xvii.21.
23. "The Evolutionary Process," in Huxley and others, eds., *Evolution as a Process*, p. 13.

24. Ephesians iv.13.
25. *Corpus Christi*, p. 47.
26. Revelation xxi.10; Ephesians v.27.
27. Bernard of Morlaix, *De Contemptu mundi* (translation by J. M. Neale, *The Rhythm of Bernard de Morlaix*, London, J. T. Hayes, 1865).
28. *Adversus Haereses*, v, 36, 3.

BIBLIOGRAPHY

Bastable, Patrick K. Desire for God. London, Burns, Oates, and Washbourne, 1947.

Bertalanffy, Ludwig von. Problems of Life. London, Watts, 1952.

Bentley, G. B. "One Flesh," *Christendom* (March, 1940).

Borne, Etienne, and François Henry. A Philosophy of Work. Translated by Francis Jackson. New York, Sheed and Ward, 1938.

Bouyer, Louis. The Spirit and Forms of Protestantism. Translated by A. V. Littledale. London, Harvill Press, 1956.

Butterfield, Herbert. The Whig Interpretation of History. London, G. Bell, 1950.

Chesterton, G. K. G. F. Watts. London, Duckworth, 1909.

Clark, W. E. Le Gros. "Structure of the Brain and the Process of Thinking," in Peter Laslett, ed., *The Physical Basis of Mind*. Oxford, Blackwell, 1950.

Demant, V. A. "Oxford Hears Billy Graham Again," *The Oxford Magazine*, LXXIV (November 24, 1955).

Dix, Gregory. The Shape of the Liturgy. London, Dacre Press, 1945.

Doms, Herbert. The Meaning of Marriage. Translated by George Sayer. New York, Sheed and Ward, 1939.

Drucker, Peter F. The Future of Industrial Man. London, Heinemann, 1943; New York, John Day, 1942.

Ducrocq, Albert. The Origins of Life. Translated by Alec Brown. London, Elek Books, 1958.

Eddington, Sir Arthur Stanley. The Nature of the Physical World. Cambridge, Cambridge University Press, 1928.

Fisher, Sir Ronald. "Retrospect of the Criticisms of the Theory of Natural Selection," in Julian Huxley and others, eds., Evolution as a Process. London, Allen and Unwin, 1954.

Gill, Eric. Beauty Looks after Herself. New York, Sheed and Ward, 1933.

—— The Necessity of Belief. London, Faber and Faber, 1936.

Gilson, Etienne. Being and Some Philosophers. Toronto, Pontifical Institute of Medieval Studies, 1949.

—— The Christian Philosophy of St. Thomas Aquinas. Translated by L. K. Shook. New York, Random House, 1956.

—— The Spirit of Medieval Philosophy. Translated by A. H. C. Downes. London, Sheed and Ward, 1936.

Heydon, J. K. World D. New York, London, Sheed and Ward, 1935.

Hildebrand, Dietrich von. Die Ehe. Munich, J. Müller, 1929.

Hoyle, Fred. Frontiers of Astronomy. New York, Harper, 1955.

Huxley, Julian Sorrel. "The Evolutionary Process," in Julian Huxley and others, eds., Evolution as a Process. London, Allen and Unwin, 1954.

—— The Uniqueness of Man. London, Chatto and Windus, 1941.

Lewis, Clive Staples. Arthurian Torso. London, Oxford University Press, 1948.

—— Out of the Silent Planet. London, John Lane, 1940.

—— Perelandra. London, John Lane, 1943.

—— The Screwtape Letters. London, G. Bles, 1942.

—— "The Weight of Glory," Theology (November, 1941).

Lossky, Vladimir. The Mystical Theology of the Eastern Church. Translated by members of the Fellowship of St. Alban and St. Sergius. London, Clarke, 1957.

Lubac, Henri de. Surnaturel. Paris, Aubier, 1946.

Mackintosh, H. R. Types of Modern Theology. London, Nisbet, 1937.

Maréchal, Joseph. Studies in the Psychology of the Mystics. Translated by Algar Thorold. New York, Benziger, 1927.

Maritain, Jacques. Religion and Culture. Translated by J. F. Scanlan. London, Sheed and Ward, 1931.

—— Scholasticism and Politics. Translated by Mortimer J. Adler. New York, Macmillan, 1940.

—— True Humanism. Translated by M. R. Adamson. London, Bles, 1938.

Mascall, Eric Lionel. Christian Theology and Natural Science. London, Longmans, Green, 1956.

—— Christ, the Christian, and the Church. London, Longmans, Green, 1946.

—— Corpus Christi. London, Longmans, Green, 1953.

—— "The Person and the Family," in Maurice B. Reckitt, ed., Prospect for Christendom. London, Faber and Faber, 1945.

—— The Recovery of Unity. London, Longmans, Green, 1958.

—— Via Media. London, Longmans, Green, 1956.

Mersch, Emile. "Filii in Filio," Nouvelle Revue théologique (July, 1938).

—— Love, Marriage, and Chastity. Translated by A. B. New York, Sheed and Ward, 1939.

Niebuhr, Reinhold. Moral Man and Immoral Society. New York, Scribner, 1932.

Nygren, Anders. Agape and Eros. 3 vols. Authorized translation by Philip S. Watson. London, Society for promoting Christian Knowledge. New York, Macmillan, 1953.

O'Mahony, James E. The Desire of God in the Philosophy of St. Thomas Aquinas. Dublin and Cork, Cork University Press, 1929.

Paul, Leslie Allen. Nature into History. London, Faber and Faber, 1957.

Pieper, Josef. The Silence of St. Thomas. Translated by John Murray and Daniel O'Connor. New York, Pantheon, 1957.

Raven, C. E. Natural Religion and Christian Theology. 2 vols. Cambridge, Cambridge University Press, 1953.

Reckitt, Maurice B. "The Preservation of Marriage," Christendom (December, 1937).

Soloviev, Vladimir Sergeevich. The Meaning of Love. Trans-
    lated by Jane Marshall. New York, International Universities
    Press, 1947.
Teilhard de Chardin, Pierre. Le Phénomène humain. Paris, Edi-
    tions du Seuil, 1955.
Thompson, William Robert. Science and Common Sense. Lon-
    don, Longmans, Green, 1937.
Thornton, Lionel Spencer. The Incarnate Lord. London, Long-
    mans, Green, 1928.
—— Revelation and the Modern World. London, Dacre Press,
    1950.
Waddington, C. H. The Scientific Attitude. New York, Penguin
    Books, 1941.
Ward, Maisie. Gilbert Keith Chesterton. New York, Sheed and
    Ward, 1943.
Wayne, T. G. Morals and Marriage. London, Longmans, Green,
    1936.
Whitrow, G. J. The Structure of the Universe. London, Hutch-
    inson's University Library, 1949.